EAT MORE

GREENS

Eat More Plants with Over
65 Quick and Easy Recipes

FERN GREEN

photography by Kirstie Young

EAT MORE

GREENS

Eat More Plants with Over
65 Quick and Easy Recipes

Hardie Grant

BOOKS

CONTENTS

INTRODUCTION

We all know that eating plants is good for us, but what do we know about eating large varieties of plants and why this is better? Plant-based food consists of fruits, vegetables, wholegrains, pulses, legumes, nuts, seeds and even herbs and spices. How many of these whole plant foods do you consume each week? Thirty maybe?

Research has shown that people who eat over 30 plants a week have a greater diverse gut microbiome than those who only eat 10 a week. Dr Tim Spector from the British Gut Project ran a DNA analysis from the microbiome of 10,000 people and found that those eating 30 different types of plants a week had optimum gut health. Many recent studies are discovering that gut health relates to the whole body including mental health, so if your gut health is good, then your brain function, heart health and immunity will follow.

We can all get into a rut when it comes to our eating habits. Our lifestyles are busy, and time that we spend on creating meals can be limited. We are probably all guilty of eating the same plants each week, but if we do this regularly, over time the diversity of our gut bacteria will shrink, which can cause repercussions to our health. Research has suggested that bad gut health can lead to inflammatory bowel disease, autoimmune disease, Type 2 diabetes and cancer.

This book is full of tips on how to increase your weekly intake of plants with delicious simple recipes that you will enjoy. Showcasing popular family meals, cooking in one pot and creating nourishing bowls to increase your plant fibre, use this book as a helpful reference guide when you need some plant-boosting inspiration.

WHY THE BIG 30?

We can be creatures of habit. When we visit our local supermarket or shop online we have a tendency to choose the same foods regularly. To increase our plant diversity, we don't need to make our meals more complicated or expensive; simple recipes are the best and increasing your plant intake is a lot easier than you think.

5-A-DAY RULE

When thinking about increasing plants and essentially fibre into your diet, the 5-a-day rule is a good place to start. However, this rule does not take into account the trillions of microbes that are living in the gut. These microbes need different types of plant foods to flourish, so varying your recipes and working with the seasons can help you change up your plant diversity.

WHAT ARE THE BENEFITS OF FIBRE?

Within our gut microbiome, limiting our diet limits our bacteria, which in turn, restricts our health. Our food is their food. If we cut out a whole food group, microbes that thrive on that food will starve into extinction. They procreate so quickly that the food choices we make in 24 hours will alter the evolution of 50 generations of microbes. It doesn't take days or even weeks to change our microbes, it takes just one bite.

Did you know that 90 per cent of us are not getting enough fibre in our diet? We need to consume 30 g (1 oz) per day as part of a healthy diet, which can be a hard number to hit when you think a medium apple is only 2.1 g. Luckily, nature has packaged both soluble and insoluble fibres into lots of plant-based foods, so variety is key.

INCREASING YOUR FIBRE INTAKE:

 Bulks out and softens stools by retaining water, which supports bowel movement and prevents constipation.

 Certain types of fibre can be fermented by beneficial gut bacteria, which leads to happy microbes.

 Can help keep you feeling fuller for longer and ultimately help you lose weight.

 Increases microbe 'skills' to train the immune cells, which improves our resilience to fight infection.

 Helps to strengthens the gut barrier and communicates with our brain.

 Helps balance blood sugar levels, which in turn increases energy levels.

 Lowers blood fats.

 Reduces risk of developing high cholesterol, heart disease, diabetes and bowel cancer.

TOP 10 PLANT FOODS THAT ARE HIGH IN FIBRE

Some of these foods may come as a surprise. Use this list when shopping, as it is always good to have a few of these in your weekly meal plan.

1. Beans

Lentils and other beans are an easy way to add fibre to your diet. Add them to soups, stews and salads. They also contain a good source of plant protein, which helps keep you feeling fuller for longer.

2. Broccoli

Broccoli is from the brassica family, along with cauliflower and kale. They are all rich in fibre. Studies have shown that broccoli's 2.8 g fibre per 100 g (3½ oz) may support gut bacteria to help you stay healthy.

3. Berries

Berries are high in antioxidants and fibre – 80 g (2¾ oz) blueberries contain 1.2 g fibre. This is similar in 80 g (2¾ oz) frozen blueberries. Blackberries and strawberries are great sources of fibre.

4. Avocados

As well as having a big dose of healthy fats, avocados are also high in fibre – half an average avocado contains 2.6 g fibre. They are great to use in salad dressings as well as making ice creams very creamy.

5. Wholegrains

These consist of wholemeal bread, wholemeal pasta and grains, such as millet, quinoa and freekeh. Don't forget that oats are also full of fibre – 50 g (1¾ oz/ ½ cup) oats contains 4 g fibre.

6. Apples

This delicious fruit comes in all sorts of varieties, so they are great as a snack and can increase your fibre amount – there's 2.4 g fibre in 1 medium apple.

7. Dried Fruits

Figs, prunes and dates are all good at increasing your fibre intake and they are a popular choice for those struggling with constipation. Just don't eat too many in one sitting as it may have the opposite effect!

8. Potatoes

Sweet, red, purple or plain potatoes are all good sources of fibre. Keep the skins on to reach your fibre goals at 3 g per potato.

9. Nuts and Seeds

These are a super source of fibre, protein and healthy fats. Sunflower seeds and almonds provide nearly 3 g fibre in a serving. Nut butter packs a punch too – but try to avoid salted varieties.

10. Popcorn

This is definitely surprising! There is a generous amount of fibre hiding in their airy, light, popped kernels. It is great for snacking on and simple to make.

IMPROVING GUT HEALTH

Good gut health does not need to be time consuming, it is all about adding rather than restricting your foods. Try these four helpful food hacks to eat 30 plants in a week.

1. Using tinned or dried lentils, beans and chickpeas are an easy win. They are great for bulking out and adding to fresh food to help it go further.

2. Use your freezer. Buy mixed frozen vegetables and fruits and freeze stewed apples, sliced bananas and berries to increase your intake easily.

3. Replace shop-bought sauces for homemade ones (page 70).

4. Try to avoid processed food.

INCREASING YOUR PLANT FIBRE

Here are some easy ways to increase your fibre intake and feed your gut:

Try using wholemeal, lentil, chickpea and brown rice pasta instead of regular pasta.

Eat wholegrain sourdough instead of white bread.

Replace white rice with brown rice, red rice and wild rice. Mix your rice with beans for added fibre.

The more you increase your fibre, the more water you need to consume; up to 1.5 litres (50 fl oz/ 6 cups) a day.

CALCULATING PLANT POINTS

Every plant counts as 1 point. Herbs also count as 1 plant point each. In this book, the plant count is recorded for each recipe.

MENU PLANNING

Use this menu plan as a guide. Each day has a suggested recipe, either breakfast, lunch or dinner, so you just need to think about your plant intake once a day and not in every meal.

	week 1	week 2	week 3	week 4
Monday	Porridge (page 14) lunch dinner	breakfast Vegetable Fritters (page 62) dinner	breakfast lunch Spiced Cod (page 72)	Overnight Oats (page 18) lunch dinner
Tuesday	breakfast Minestrone Pasta (page 68) dinner	breakfast lunch Lasagne (page 106)	Scrambled Egg (page 60) lunch dinner	breakfast Feta Parcels (page 36) dinner
Wednesday	breakfast lunch Chicken Curry (page 76)	Power Smoothie (page 134) lunch dinner	breakfast Tuna Salad (page 32) dinner	breakfast lunch Tacos (page 74)
Thursday	Smoothie Bowl (page 16) lunch dinner	breakfast Chicken Balls (page 30) dinner	breakfast lunch Ragu (page 78)	Granola (page 102) lunch dinner
Friday	breakfast Shakshuka (page 58) dinner	breakfast lunch Baked Peppers (page 110)	Green Smoothie (page 140) lunch dinner	breakfast Halloumi Salad (page 42) dinner
Saturday	breakfast lunch Baked Lamb (page 112)	Avocado Smoothie (page 146) lunch dinner	breakfast Potato Salad (page 38) dinner	breakfast lunch Pizza (page 116)
Sunday	Pancakes (page 56) lunch dinner	breakfast Mac 'n' Cheese (page 66) dinner	breakfast lunch Risotto (page 84)	Morning Smoothie (page 136) lunch dinner
TOTAL PLANT POINTS	55	46	53	59

NOURISH BOWLS

Nourish bowls can be anything from hearty soups to big colourful salads. They take on a number of plant-based foods using wholegrains and a wide range of legumes, nuts and seeds to fill you up with fibre and keep your taste buds satisfied while packing that plant-based punch.

PORRIDGE

Increase your plant count with this delicious bowl of goodness. The multigrain flakes with mixed poached fruits will fill you up and warm the soul.

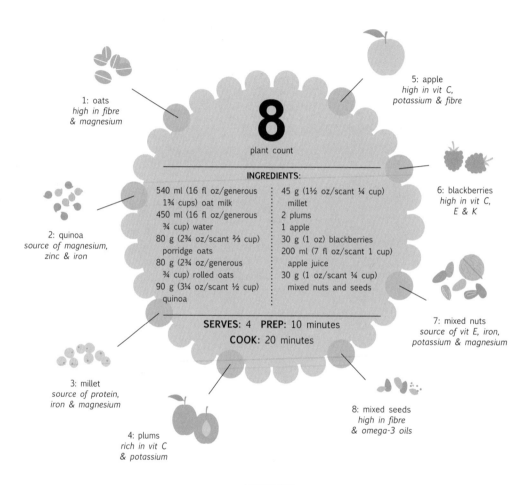

1: oats
*high in fibre
& magnesium*

2: quinoa
*source of magnesium,
zinc & iron*

3: millet
*source of protein,
iron & magnesium*

4: plums
*rich in vit C
& potassium*

5: apple
*high in vit C,
potassium & fibre*

6: blackberries
*high in vit C,
E & K*

7: mixed nuts
*source of vit E, iron,
potassium & magnesium*

8: mixed seeds
*high in fibre
& omega-3 oils*

8
plant count

INGREDIENTS:

540 ml (16 fl oz/generous 1¾ cups) oat milk
450 ml (16 fl oz/generous ¾ cup) water
80 g (2¾ oz/scant ⅔ cup) porridge oats
80 g (2¾ oz/generous ¾ cup) rolled oats
90 g (3¼ oz/scant ½ cup) quinoa

45 g (1½ oz/scant ¼ cup) millet
2 plums
1 apple
30 g (1 oz) blackberries
200 ml (7 fl oz/scant 1 cup) apple juice
30 g (1 oz/scant ¼ cup) mixed nuts and seeds

SERVES: 4   **PREP:** 10 minutes
COOK: 20 minutes

METHOD:

1 Combine the milk with 450 ml (16 fl oz/generous ¾ cup) water with the oats, quinoa and millet in a saucepan. **2** Bring to the boil, then reduce the heat to low and cook for 20 minutes, stirring occasionally until all the grains are softened.
3 Meanwhile, add the quartered plums and thinly sliced apple to another pan with the blackberries and apple juice. **4** Bring to the boil, then turn off the heat and leave until the porridge is ready. **5** Serve the porridge topped with the fruit, nuts and seeds.

SMOOTHIE BOWL

Whip up this simple smoothie bowl and feel free to swap the berries and use
the fruit you already have. Your gut is interested in variety, so keep it fed
with colourful fruits.

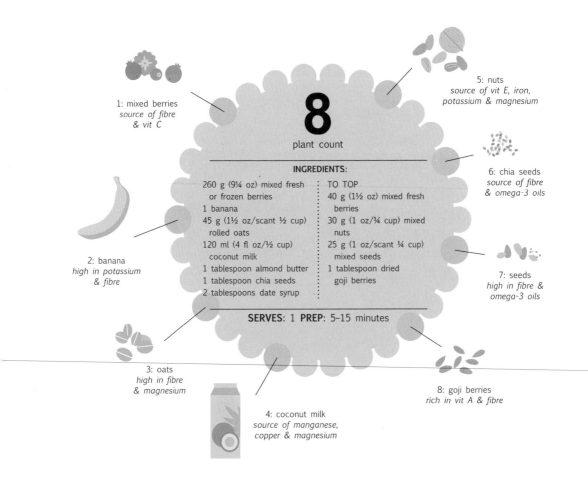

1: mixed berries
*source of fibre
& vit C*

5: nuts
*source of vit E, iron,
potassium & magnesium*

8
plant count

6: chia seeds
*source of fibre
& omega-3 oils*

INGREDIENTS:

260 g (9¼ oz) mixed fresh
or frozen berries
1 banana
45 g (1½ oz/scant ½ cup)
rolled oats
120 ml (4 fl oz/½ cup)
coconut milk
1 tablespoon almond butter
1 tablespoon chia seeds
2 tablespoons date syrup

TO TOP
40 g (1½ oz) mixed fresh
berries
30 g (1 oz/¼ cup) mixed
nuts
25 g (1 oz/scant ¼ cup)
mixed seeds
1 tablespoon dried
goji berries

2: banana
*high in potassium
& fibre*

7: seeds
*high in fibre &
omega-3 oils*

SERVES: 1 PREP: 5–15 minutes

3: oats
*high in fibre
& magnesium*

8: goji berries
rich in vit A & fibre

4: coconut milk
*source of manganese,
copper & magnesium*

METHOD:

1 If using frozen berries, leave to thaw for 5–10 minutes. **2** Add the thawed
or fresh berries, peeled banana, oats, coconut milk, almond butter, chia seeds
and date syrup to a blender and whizz until smooth, but still thick. **3** Pour the
smoothie into a serving bowl and top with the fresh berries, nuts, seeds and goji
berries. Serve.

OVERNIGHT OATS

This bircher-style breakfast lends itself to many variations and can be prepared ahead of time. Try this chai-flavoured recipe with apple and stone fruits.

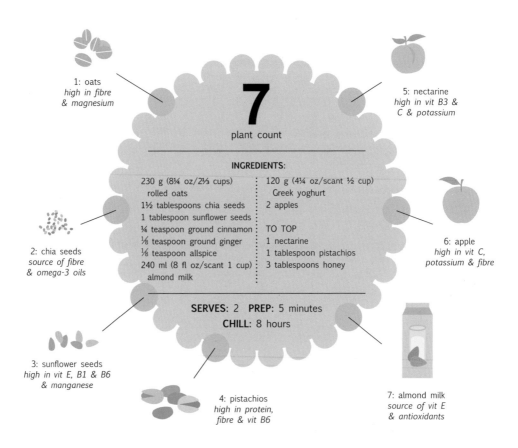

7

plant count

1: oats
*high in fibre
& magnesium*

5: nectarine
*high in vit B3 &
C & potassium*

2: chia seeds
*source of fibre
& omega-3 oils*

6: apple
*high in vit C,
potassium & fibre*

3: sunflower seeds
*high in vit E, B1 & B6
& manganese*

4: pistachios
*high in protein,
fibre & vit B6*

7: almond milk
*source of vit E
& antioxidants*

INGREDIENTS:

230 g (8¼ oz/2⅓ cups)
rolled oats
1½ tablespoons chia seeds
1 tablespoon sunflower seeds
¼ teaspoon ground cinnamon
⅛ teaspoon ground ginger
⅛ teaspoon allspice
240 ml (8 fl oz/scant 1 cup)
almond milk

120 g (4¼ oz/scant ½ cup)
Greek yoghurt
2 apples

TO TOP
1 nectarine
1 tablespoon pistachios
3 tablespoons honey

SERVES: 2 **PREP:** 5 minutes
CHILL: 8 hours

METHOD:

1 Combine the oats, seeds and spices in a large airtight container. **2** Add the almond milk and yoghurt and stir until thoroughly combined. **3** Seal with a lid and chill in the refrigerator overnight. **4** The next morning, stir in the grated apple, divide between two glasses or bowls, add the thinly sliced nectarines, pistachios and drizzle with honey to serve.

RICOTTA BALLS

Creamy ricotta balls rolled in roasted hazelnuts are super delicious with this roasted red (bell) pepper salad. Try serving it with a seedy flatbread or wholegrain pitta bread to scoop up all the juices.

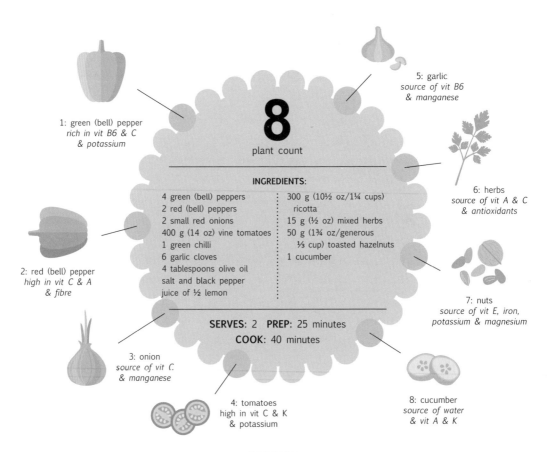

8

plant count

1: green (bell) pepper
*rich in vit B6 & C
& potassium*

5: garlic
*source of vit B6
& manganese*

6: herbs
*source of vit A & C
& antioxidants*

INGREDIENTS:

4 green (bell) peppers
2 red (bell) peppers
2 small red onions
400 g (14 oz) vine tomatoes
1 green chilli
6 garlic cloves
4 tablespoons olive oil
salt and black pepper
juice of ½ lemon

300 g (10½ oz/1¼ cups)
 ricotta
15 g (½ oz) mixed herbs
50 g (1¾ oz/generous
 ⅓ cup) toasted hazelnuts
1 cucumber

2: red (bell) pepper
*high in vit C & A
& fibre*

7: nuts
*source of vit E, iron,
potassium & magnesium*

SERVES: 2 PREP: 25 minutes
COOK: 40 minutes

3: onion
*source of vit C
& manganese*

4: tomatoes
*high in vit C & K
& potassium*

8: cucumber
*source of water
& vit A & K*

METHOD:

1 Preheat the oven to 250°C (480°F). **2** Toss the peppers, chopped into 4 cm (1½ in) pieces, chopped onions, quartered tomatoes, chilli and peeled garlic in the oil. Season. **3** Spread the vegetables out on a lined baking tray (pan) and roast until soft and charred. **4** Rest for 5 minutes, then roughly chop. **5** Stir in the lemon juice, ricotta and half the herbs, then season. **6** Roll the ricotta into balls about half the size of a golf ball. **7** Add the finely chopped hazelnuts to a bowl, then roll each ricotta ball in the nuts until covered. **8** Divide the roasted pepper mixture between two bowls, add the peeled, seeded and cubed cucumber and serve with the ricotta balls and remaining herbs.

ROAST CHICKEN SALAD

This tasty spiced salad has the secret spice ingredient of curry leaves, which bring both the aromatic flavour as well as the moreish appeal to this crunchy textured recipe.

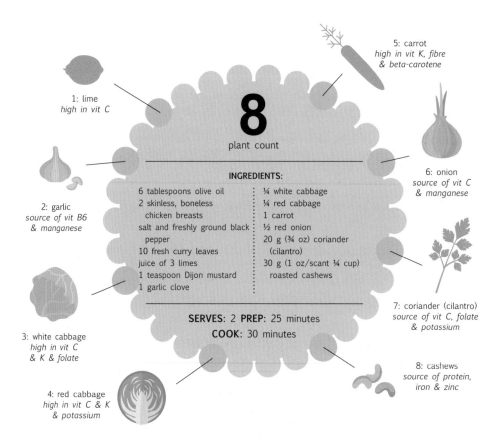

1: lime
high in vit C

2: garlic
source of vit B6
& manganese

3: white cabbage
high in vit C
& K & folate

4: red cabbage
high in vit C & K
& potassium

5: carrot
high in vit K, fibre
& beta-carotene

6: onion
source of vit C
& manganese

7: coriander (cilantro)
source of vit C, folate
& potassium

8: cashews
source of protein,
iron & zinc

8
plant count

INGREDIENTS:

6 tablespoons olive oil
2 skinless, boneless
  chicken breasts
salt and freshly ground black
  pepper
10 fresh curry leaves
juice of 3 limes
1 teaspoon Dijon mustard
1 garlic clove

¼ white cabbage
¼ red cabbage
1 carrot
½ red onion
20 g (¾ oz) coriander
  (cilantro)
30 g (1 oz/scant ¼ cup)
  roasted cashews

SERVES: 2 PREP: 25 minutes
COOK: 30 minutes

METHOD:

1 Preheat the oven to 220°C (425°F). Rub 1 teaspoon of oil over each chicken breast and season. Roast for 25–30 minutes until cooked through. **2** Heat 3 tablespoons of the oil in a frying pan for 30 seconds. **3** Add the curry leaves and cook for 2 minutes. Set aside. **4** Whisk the lime juice, mustard, grated garlic and remaining oil together to make a dressing. Season with salt; set aside. **5** Combine the finely shredded cabbage, julienned carrot and thinly sliced red onion in a large bowl; season. **6** Pour over the dressing and leave for 15 minutes to soften. **7** Fold through the chopped coriander and top with the cashews. **8** Serve the slaw with the chicken and curry leaf oil.

TOMATO BROTH

Wholegrains are added to this comforting soup to increase your plant intake, and is a great trick to add to other flavoured soups.

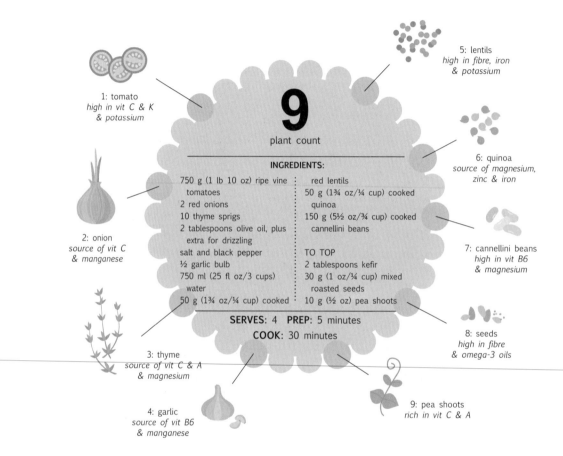

5: lentils
high in fibre, iron & potassium

1: tomato
high in vit C & K & potassium

9

plant count

6: quinoa
source of magnesium, zinc & iron

INGREDIENTS:

750 g (1 lb 10 oz) ripe vine tomatoes
2 red onions
10 thyme sprigs
2 tablespoons olive oil, plus extra for drizzling
salt and black pepper
½ garlic bulb
750 ml (25 fl oz/3 cups) water
50 g (1¾ oz/¼ cup) cooked

red lentils
50 g (1¾ oz/¼ cup) cooked quinoa
150 g (5½ oz/¾ cup) cooked cannellini beans

TO TOP
2 tablespoons kefir
30 g (1 oz/¼ cup) mixed roasted seeds
10 g (½ oz) pea shoots

SERVES: 4   PREP: 5 minutes
COOK: 30 minutes

2: onion
source of vit C & manganese

7: cannellini beans
high in vit B6 & magnesium

8: seeds
high in fibre & omega-3 oils

3: thyme
source of vit C & A & magnesium

4: garlic
source of vit B6 & manganese

9: pea shoots
rich in vit C & A

METHOD:

1 Preheat the oven to 180°C (350°F). **2** Arrange the halved tomatoes, onions and thyme on a large baking tray (pan) and toss well with oil. Season. **3** Cover the garlic in foil and put onto the tray. Roast for 30 minutes, or until the tomatoes and onions start to colour. **4** Remove and discard thyme, then add the ingredients to a blender with the water, cooked lentils, quinoa and beans. **5** Open the garlic parcel and squeeze the garlic on top. **6** Blitz for 1–2 minutes to your preferred consistency. **7** Check the seasoning, then serve with the kefir, seeds and pea shoots. Drizzle with oil to finish.

ROOT SALAD

The mix of cannellini beans and chickpeas (garbanzos) makes the hummus beautifully smooth. Double the recipe and you can use them for other dishes or a simple soup.

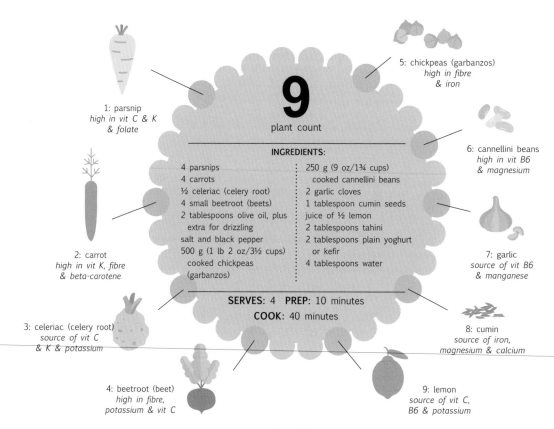

9

plant count

1: parsnip
high in vit C & K
& folate

2: carrot
high in vit K, fibre
& beta-carotene

3: celeriac (celery root)
source of vit C
& K & potassium

4: beetroot (beet)
high in fibre,
potassium & vit C

5: chickpeas (garbanzos)
high in fibre
& iron

6: cannellini beans
high in vit B6
& magnesium

7: garlic
source of vit B6
& manganese

8: cumin
source of iron,
magnesium & calcium

9: lemon
source of vit C,
B6 & potassium

INGREDIENTS:

4 parsnips
4 carrots
½ celeriac (celery root)
4 small beetroot (beets)
2 tablespoons olive oil, plus
   extra for drizzling
salt and black pepper
500 g (1 lb 2 oz/3½ cups)
   cooked chickpeas
   (garbanzos)

250 g (9 oz/1¾ cups)
   cooked cannellini beans
2 garlic cloves
1 tablespoon cumin seeds
juice of ½ lemon
2 tablespoons tahini
2 tablespoons plain yoghurt
   or kefir
4 tablespoons water

SERVES: 4 **PREP:** 10 minutes
COOK: 40 minutes

METHOD:

1 Preheat the oven to 220°C (425°F). **2** Arrange the quartered parsnips, halved carrots, peeled celeriac, cut into 4 cm (1½ in) chunks, and halved beetroot on a lined baking tray (pan), drizzle with oil and season. **3** Roast for 40 minutes, or until the vegetables are charred and cooked through. **4** Add the chickpeas, beans, garlic, cumin, lemon juice, tahini, yoghurt and water to a blender and whizz until smooth. Season with salt. Add more water to reach desired consistency. **5** Pour into a small pan and warm through gently. **6** Once the vegetables are roasted, divide the warm hummus among four serving bowls and top with the vegetables. Drizzle with oil.

VEGETABLE SOUP

This warming bowl of soup has everything you need on a cold winter's day.
Enjoy the dukkah (Middle Eastern hazelnut spice mix) toasts to dip leisurely.

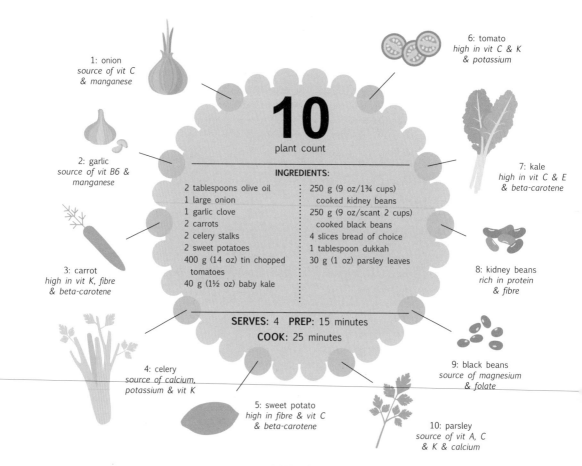

1: onion
*source of vit C
& manganese*

2: garlic
*source of vit B6 &
manganese*

3: carrot
*high in vit K, fibre
& beta-carotene*

4: celery
*source of calcium,
potassium & vit K*

5: sweet potato
*high in fibre & vit C
& beta-carotene*

6: tomato
*high in vit C & K
& potassium*

7: kale
*high in vit C & E
& beta-carotene*

8: kidney beans
*rich in protein
& fibre*

9: black beans
*source of magnesium
& folate*

10: parsley
*source of vit A, C
& K & calcium*

10
plant count

INGREDIENTS:

2 tablespoons olive oil
1 large onion
1 garlic clove
2 carrots
2 celery stalks
2 sweet potatoes
400 g (14 oz) tin chopped
   tomatoes
40 g (1½ oz) baby kale

250 g (9 oz/1¾ cups)
   cooked kidney beans
250 g (9 oz/scant 2 cups)
   cooked black beans
4 slices bread of choice
1 tablespoon dukkah
30 g (1 oz) parsley leaves

SERVES: 4 **PREP:** 15 minutes
COOK: 25 minutes

METHOD:

1 Heat 1 tablespoon of the oil in a large saucepan, add the diced onion and grated garlic and fry for 6–7 minutes until softened. **2** Add the diced carrots, diced celery and diced sweet potato and cook for 6–7 minutes. **3** Add the tomatoes and 1 litre (34 fl oz/4¼ cups) water and bring to the boil. **4** Once boiling, reduce the heat to low and simmer for 12 minutes. **5** Add the kale and beans and bring to the boil, then turn off the heat and cover with the lid. **6** Grill (broil) your favourite bread, then drizzle the toast with the remaining oil and sprinkle with dukkah. Garnish the soup with chopped parsley.

CHICKEN BALLS

Tasty miso-style sesame meatballs go hand in hand with this colourful slaw.
Make sure the chicken thighs are skinless and boneless.

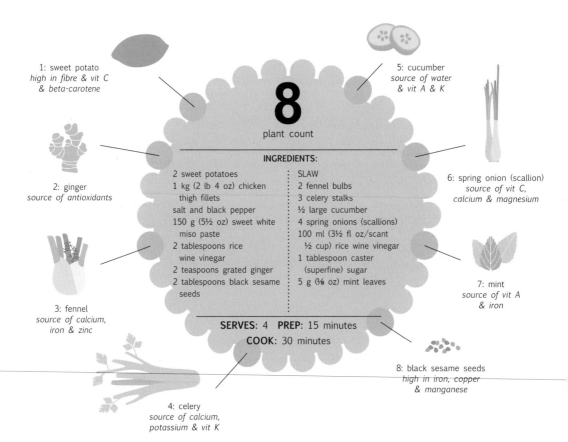

1: sweet potato
*high in fibre & vit C
& beta-carotene*

5: cucumber
*source of water
& vit A & K*

8
plant count

2: ginger
source of antioxidants

6: spring onion (scallion)
*source of vit C,
calcium & magnesium*

INGREDIENTS:

2 sweet potatoes
1 kg (2 lb 4 oz) chicken
  thigh fillets
salt and black pepper
150 g (5½ oz) sweet white
  miso paste
2 tablespoons rice
  wine vinegar
2 teaspoons grated ginger
2 tablespoons black sesame
  seeds

SLAW
2 fennel bulbs
3 celery stalks
½ large cucumber
4 spring onions (scallions)
100 ml (3½ fl oz/scant
  ½ cup) rice wine vinegar
1 tablespoon caster
  (superfine) sugar
5 g (⅛ oz) mint leaves

7: mint
*source of vit A
& iron*

3: fennel
*source of calcium,
iron & zinc*

SERVES: 4 **PREP:** 15 minutes
COOK: 30 minutes

8: black sesame seeds
*high in iron, copper
& manganese*

4: celery
*source of calcium,
potassium & vit K*

METHOD:

1 Preheat the oven to 200°C (400°F). **2** Bake the sweet potatoes for 30 minutes.
3 Meanwhile, add the chicken, skinned and boned and cut into chunks, with pinch of
salt to a food processor and pulse until smooth. **4** Roll the mixture into small balls.
5 Mix the miso, vinegar and ginger together, then use to coat each ball, placing
each on a lined baking sheet. **6** Sprinkle with sesame seeds. **7** Roast for 15 minutes.
8 For the slaw, slice the fennel finely and drop into a bowl of water. **9** Finely slice
the celery, cucumber and spring onions and add to a bowl. **10** Mix the vinegar and
sugar together and pour over the vegetables. **11** Add the fennel and mint, season
and mix. Serve with the sweet potato and miso balls.

TUNA SALAD

Make this salad in minutes using sunflower and chia seeds. It is great served on sourdough for added crunch.

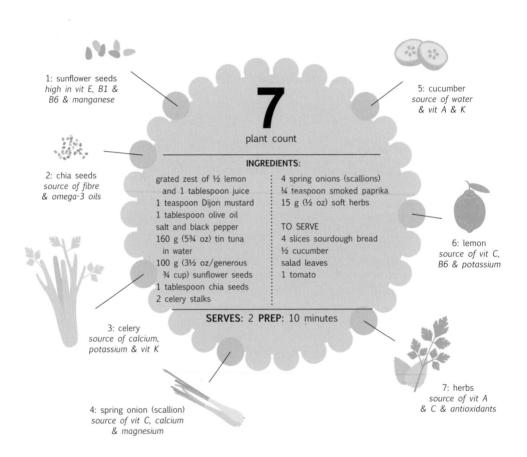

1: sunflower seeds
*high in vit E, B1 &
B6 & manganese*

2: chia seeds
*source of fibre
& omega-3 oils*

3: celery
*source of calcium,
potassium & vit K*

4: spring onion (scallion)
*source of vit C, calcium
& magnesium*

5: cucumber
*source of water
& vit A & K*

6: lemon
*source of vit C,
B6 & potassium*

7: herbs
*source of vit A
& C & antioxidants*

7
plant count

INGREDIENTS:

grated zest of ½ lemon
and 1 tablespoon juice
1 teaspoon Dijon mustard
1 tablespoon olive oil
salt and black pepper
160 g (5¾ oz) tin tuna
in water
100 g (3½ oz/generous
¾ cup) sunflower seeds
1 tablespoon chia seeds
2 celery stalks

4 spring onions (scallions)
¼ teaspoon smoked paprika
15 g (½ oz) soft herbs

TO SERVE
4 slices sourdough bread
½ cucumber
salad leaves
1 tomato

SERVES: 2 **PREP:** 10 minutes

METHOD:

1 Add the grated lemon zest and juice, mustard and oil to a jam jar, season, seal with the lid and shake until emulsfied. Set aside. **2** Add the drained tuna, seeds, chopped celery and sliced spring onions to a large bowl and sprinkle with the paprika and chopped herbs. Season and stir with a fork until combined. **3** Pour over the dressing, stir, then leave to stand. **4** Toast the sourdough, then add the cucumber, peeled into ribbons, salad leaves and sliced tomato on the top. Spoon the tuna mix on each and serve.

CHICKEN MISO

Simple to create and great on flavour, this buckwheat savoury noodle bowl of goodness can be made in minutes.

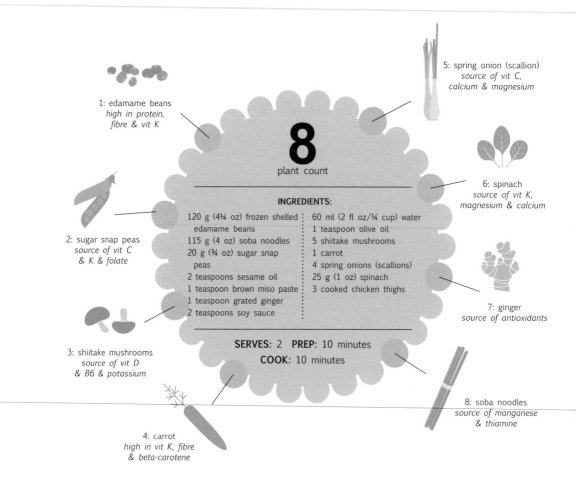

8
plant count

1: edamame beans
high in protein, fibre & vit K

2: sugar snap peas
source of vit C & K & folate

3: shiitake mushrooms
source of vit D & B6 & potassium

4: carrot
high in vit K, fibre & beta-carotene

5: spring onion (scallion)
source of vit C, calcium & magnesium

6: spinach
source of vit K, magnesium & calcium

7: ginger
source of antioxidants

8: soba noodles
source of manganese & thiamine

INGREDIENTS:

120 g (4¼ oz) frozen shelled edamame beans
115 g (4 oz) soba noodles
20 g (¾ oz) sugar snap peas
2 teaspoons sesame oil
1 teaspoon brown miso paste
1 teaspoon grated ginger
2 teaspoons soy sauce

60 ml (2 fl oz/¼ cup) water
1 teaspoon olive oil
5 shiitake mushrooms
1 carrot
4 spring onions (scallions)
25 g (1 oz) spinach
3 cooked chicken thighs

SERVES: 2   PREP: 10 minutes
COOK: 10 minutes

METHOD:

1 Bring a saucepan of water to the boil, add the edamame beans and noodles and cook for 2 minutes. **2** Add the sugar snap peas, sliced in half, to the pan and cook for 1 minute. Drain and rinse under cold water. Set aside. **3** Whisk the sesame oil, miso, ginger, soy and 60 ml (2 fl oz/¼ cup) water together. Set aside. **4** Heat the olive oil in a pan, add the sliced mushrooms, carrot, shaved into ribbons, sliced spring onions and spinach and toss and cook for 3 minutes, or until tender. **5** Add the chicken, meat pulled off the bone, and cook for 1 minute. **6** Add the noodle mixture and dressing and toss for 2–3 minutes until hot. Serve.

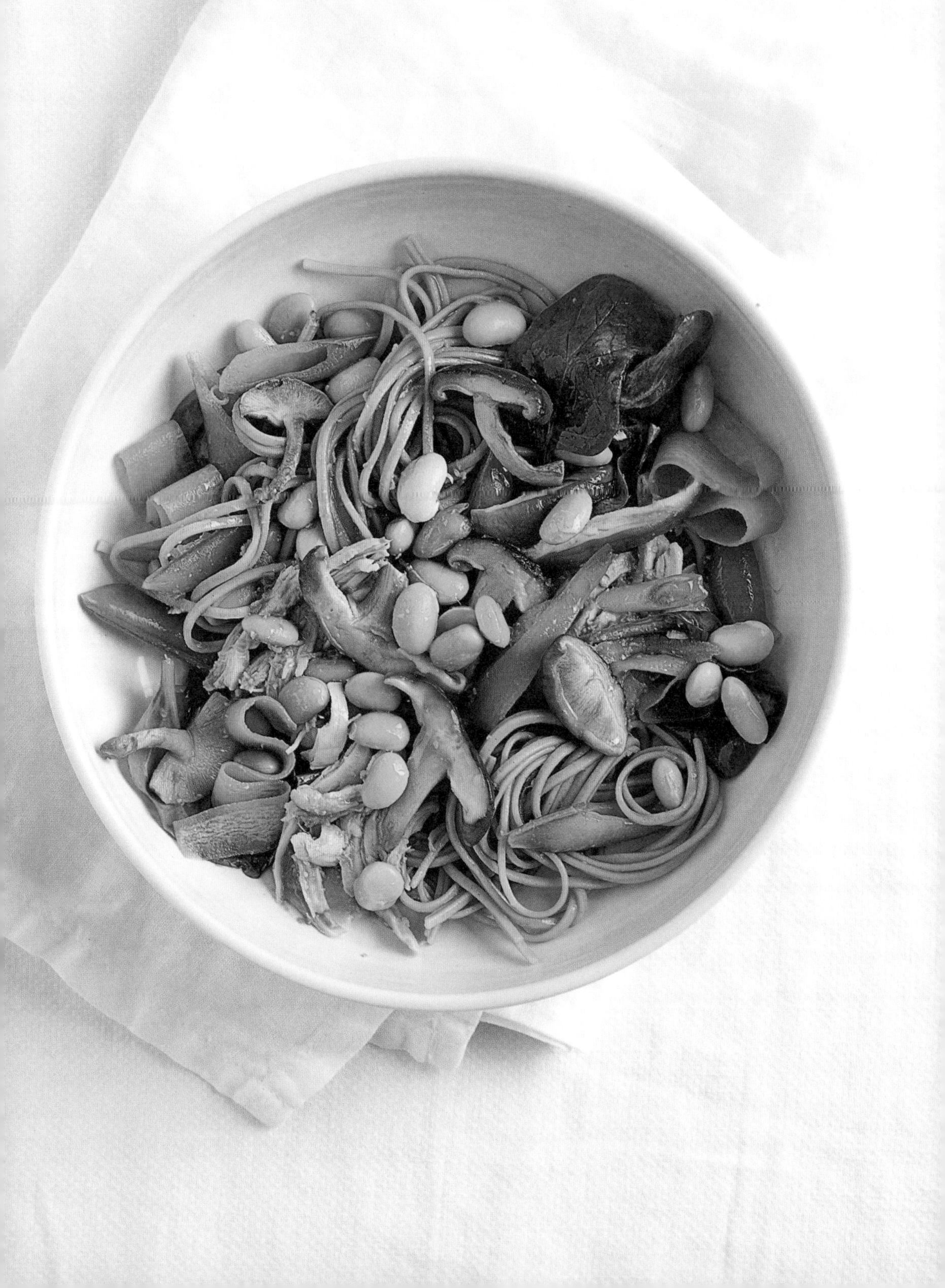

FETA PARCELS

Serve these feta parcels with a super summer grain salad. We are using farro here, which you can cook ahead of time, as it can last in the refrigerator for up to five days.

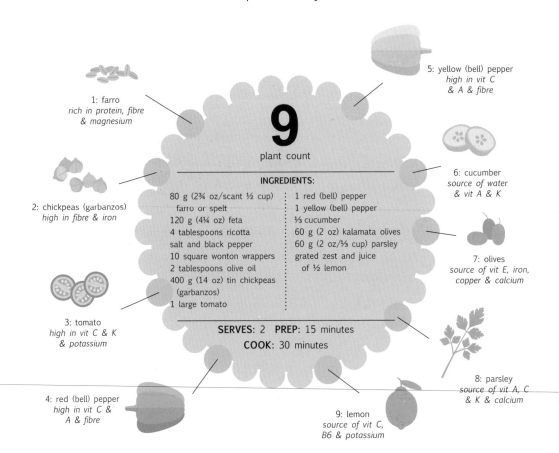

5: yellow (bell) pepper
*high in vit C
& A & fibre*

1: farro
*rich in protein, fibre
& magnesium*

9

plant count

6: cucumber
*source of water
& vit A & K*

2: chickpeas (garbanzos)
high in fibre & iron

INGREDIENTS:

80 g (2¾ oz/scant ½ cup)
  farro or spelt
120 g (4¼ oz) feta
4 tablespoons ricotta
salt and black pepper
10 square wonton wrappers
2 tablespoons olive oil
400 g (14 oz) tin chickpeas
  (garbanzos)
1 large tomato

1 red (bell) pepper
1 yellow (bell) pepper
⅓ cucumber
60 g (2 oz) kalamata olives
60 g (2 oz/⅓ cup) parsley
grated zest and juice
  of ½ lemon

7: olives
*source of vit E, iron,
copper & calcium*

3: tomato
*high in vit C & K
& potassium*

SERVES: 2   **PREP: 15 minutes**

COOK: 30 minutes

8: parsley
*source of vit A, C
& K & calcium*

4: red (bell) pepper
*high in vit C &
A & fibre*

9: lemon
*source of vit C,
B6 & potassium*

METHOD:

1 Add the farro to a large saucepan, cover with water and bring to a simmer. Cook for 25–30 minutes until tender. **2** Whisk the crumbled feta and ricotta together. Season. **3** Add 1 teaspoon of the cheese mix into the corner of a wrapper, then fold the wrapper to form a triangular parcel. Repeat with the remaining wrappers. **4** Heat the oil in a frying pan and fry the parcels for 1 minute on each side until crispy. **5** Mix the drained chickpeas, diced tomato, diced red and yellow peppers, seeded and diced cucumber, olives, chopped parsley and grated lemon zest and juice together. Add the farro. Serve with feta parcels.

POTATO SALAD

A zipped up potato salad with lots of fresh herbs. Add the sauerkraut and you have got yourself a super plant simple salad. If using ordinary sauerkraut, then add ½ teaspoon ground turmeric.

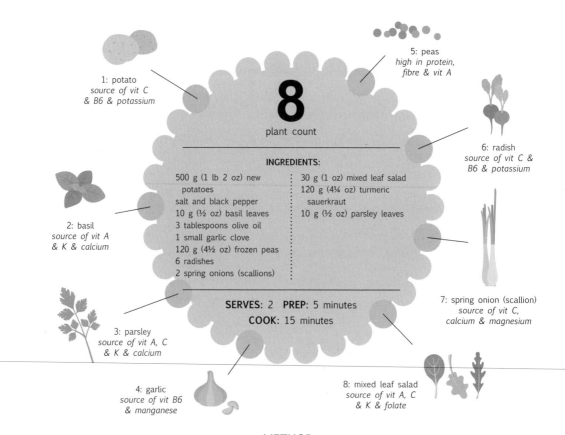

1: potato
source of vit C & B6 & potassium

5: peas
high in protein, fibre & vit A

6: radish
source of vit C & B6 & potassium

2: basil
source of vit A & K & calcium

3: parsley
source of vit A, C & K & calcium

7: spring onion (scallion)
source of vit C, calcium & magnesium

4: garlic
source of vit B6 & manganese

8: mixed leaf salad
source of vit A, C & K & folate

8
plant count

INGREDIENTS:

500 g (1 lb 2 oz) new potatoes
salt and black pepper
10 g (½ oz) basil leaves
3 tablespoons olive oil
1 small garlic clove
120 g (4½ oz) frozen peas
6 radishes
2 spring onions (scallions)

30 g (1 oz) mixed leaf salad
120 g (4¼ oz) turmeric sauerkraut
10 g (½ oz) parsley leaves

SERVES: 2 **PREP:** 5 minutes
COOK: 15 minutes

METHOD:

1 Add the potatoes to a large saucepan of salted water and bring to the boil. **2** Using a slotted spoon, add the basil leaves to the boiling water for 2 seconds to blanch, then lay on paper towels and squeeze out the excess water. **3** Whizz the basil, oil and garlic in a blender until smooth. **4** Boil the potatoes for 15 minutes, or until tender, adding the frozen peas for the last 3 minutes for cooking. **5** Drain the peas and potatoes and add them to a bowl. **6** Pour over the basil oil and stir through. **7** Divide the sliced radishes, sliced spring onions, salad, sauerkraut and chopped parsley between two bowls and top with potatoes. Season and serve.

THAI SALMON SALAD

Packed full of rainbow vegetables and served with a super tasty peanut sauce, this is best served at room temperature. It is also great in a lunch box.

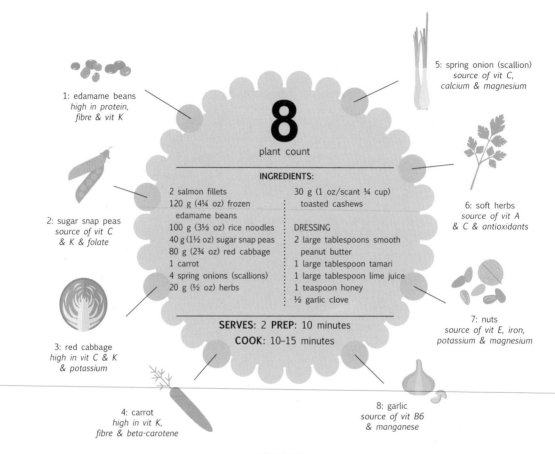

1: edamame beans
high in protein, fibre & vit K

2: sugar snap peas
source of vit C & K & folate

3: red cabbage
high in vit C & K & potassium

4: carrot
high in vit K, fibre & beta-carotene

5: spring onion (scallion)
source of vit C, calcium & magnesium

6: soft herbs
source of vit A & C & antioxidants

7: nuts
source of vit E, iron, potassium & magnesium

8: garlic
source of vit B6 & manganese

8
plant count

INGREDIENTS:

2 salmon fillets
120 g (4¼ oz) frozen edamame beans
100 g (3½ oz) rice noodles
40 g (1½ oz) sugar snap peas
80 g (2¾ oz) red cabbage
1 carrot
4 spring onions (scallions)
20 g (½ oz) herbs

30 g (1 oz/scant ¼ cup) toasted cashews

DRESSING
2 large tablespoons smooth peanut butter
1 large tablespoon tamari
1 large tablespoon lime juice
1 teaspoon honey
½ garlic clove

SERVES: 2 PREP: 10 minutes
COOK: 10–15 minutes

METHOD:

1 Preheat the oven to 200°C (400°F). **2** Bake the salmon for 10–15 minutes until just opaque and flakes easily. Set aside. **3** For the dressing, whisk the peanut butter, tamari, lime juice, honey, grated garlic with 2 tablespoons of water. Set aside.
4 Bring a large saucepan of water to the boil, add the edamame beans and cook for 3 minutes. **5** Use the cooking water to soak the noodles for 6 minutes, or until tender. **6** Add the edamame beans, sugar snaps, sliced cabbage, carrot, shaved into ribbons, sliced spring onions and herbs to a large bowl, and using two forks, mix with the noodles until combined. **7** Divide between two plates, then add the salmon, drizzle over the dressing and sprinkle with cashews.

HALLOUMI SALAD

Serve this salad with red cabbage and wintery citrus fruits to brighten up the winter palate.

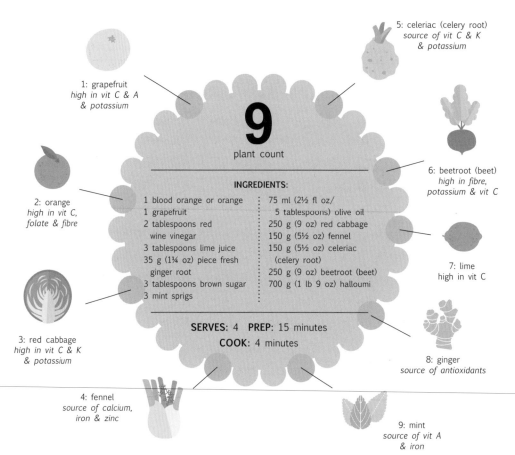

5: celeriac (celery root)
*source of vit C & K
& potassium*

1: grapefruit
*high in vit C & A
& potassium*

9
plant count

6: beetroot (beet)
*high in fibre,
potassium & vit C*

2: orange
*high in vit C,
folate & fibre*

INGREDIENTS:

1 blood orange or orange
1 grapefruit
2 tablespoons red
  wine vinegar
3 tablespoons lime juice
35 g (1¼ oz) piece fresh
  ginger root
3 tablespoons brown sugar
3 mint sprigs

75 ml (2½ fl oz/
  5 tablespoons) olive oil
250 g (9 oz) red cabbage
150 g (5½ oz) fennel
150 g (5½ oz) celeriac
  (celery root)
250 g (9 oz) beetroot (beet)
700 g (1 lb 9 oz) halloumi

7: lime
high in vit C

SERVES: 4 PREP: 15 minutes
COOK: 4 minutes

3: red cabbage
*high in vit C & K
& potassium*

8: ginger
source of antioxidants

4: fennel
*source of calcium,
iron & zinc*

9: mint
*source of vit A
& iron*

METHOD:

1 Remove the peel and pith from the orange and grapefruit, saving as much juice as you can. Segment each fruit and add to a bowl with the fruit juice. **2** Add the vinegar, lime juice, grated ginger, sugar, finely shredded mint leaves and most of the oil to the bowl and whisk together. **3** Add the thinly sliced cabbage, thinly sliced fennel, celeriac, cut into long thin matchsticks, and beetroot, cut into long thin matchsticks, to a bowl and stir well. **4** Pour over the dressing and leave to stand. **5** Brush the halloumi, cut into 1 cm (½ in) thick chunks, with the remaining oil. **6** Heat a griddle pan and cook the halloumi for 4 minutes on each side.
7 Serve the dressed vegetables with the halloumi.

HERB CREAM LINGUINE

You can't get more of a comfort bowl than this. Try using brown rice, wholegrain or farro-style pasta for an extra plant point.

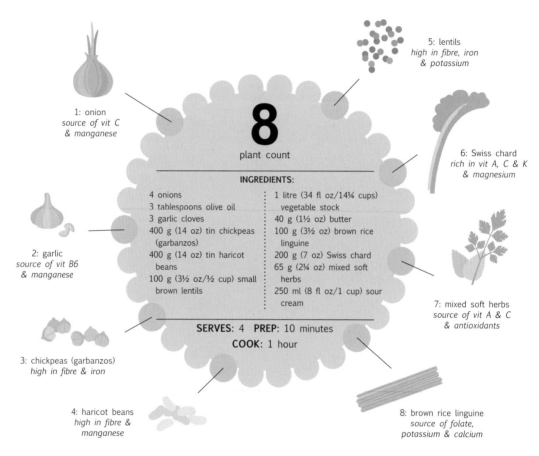

5: lentils
high in fibre, iron & potassium

1: onion
source of vit C & manganese

8

plant count

6: Swiss chard
rich in vit A, C & K & magnesium

INGREDIENTS:

4 onions
3 tablespoons olive oil
3 garlic cloves
400 g (14 oz) tin chickpeas (garbanzos)
400 g (14 oz) tin haricot beans
100 g (3½ oz/½ cup) small brown lentils

1 litre (34 fl oz/14¼ cups) vegetable stock
40 g (1½ oz) butter
100 g (3½ oz) brown rice linguine
200 g (7 oz) Swiss chard
65 g (2¼ oz) mixed soft herbs
250 ml (8 fl oz/1 cup) sour cream

SERVES: 4 **PREP:** 10 minutes
COOK: 1 hour

2: garlic
source of vit B6 & manganese

7: mixed soft herbs
source of vit A & C & antioxidants

3: chickpeas (garbanzos)
high in fibre & iron

4: haricot beans
high in fibre & manganese

8: brown rice linguine
source of folate, potassium & calcium

METHOD:

1 Roughly chop two onions. **2** Heat the oil in a large saucepan and fry the onions until softened and pale gold. **3** Stir in the grated garlic and cook for 2 minutes. **4** Add the drained chickpeas, beans, lentils and stock and bring to the boil. Reduce the heat and simmer for 30 minutes. **5** Slice the remaining onions. **6** Melt the butter in a frying pan gently, add the onions and fry for 30 minutes, or until a deep brown colour. Set aside. **7** Add the pasta and roughly chopped chard to the simmering stock and cook the pasta according to the pack instructions. **8** For the last minute, add most of the chopped herbs and fold in the sour cream. Serve, garnished with the remaining herbs and fried onions.

GRAIN BOWL

This Korean-inspired bowl of plants can be diverse in itself. Mix up the grains, change the vegetables and see what's in the cupboard.

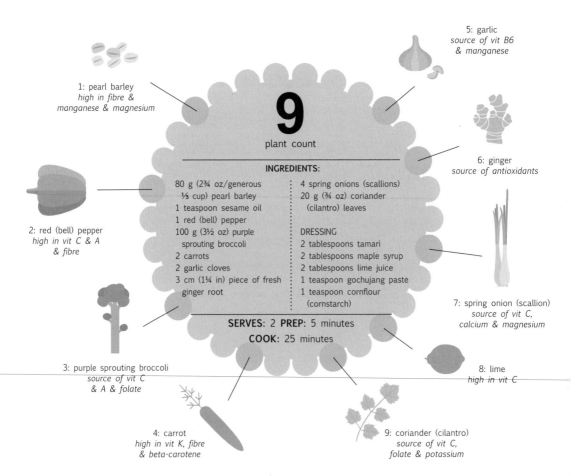

5: garlic
*source of vit B6
& manganese*

1: pearl barley
*high in fibre &
manganese & magnesium*

9
plant count

6: ginger
source of antioxidants

INGREDIENTS:

80 g (2¾ oz/generous
⅓ cup) pearl barley
1 teaspoon sesame oil
1 red (bell) pepper
100 g (3½ oz) purple
  sprouting broccoli
2 carrots
2 garlic cloves
3 cm (1¼ in) piece of fresh
  ginger root

4 spring onions (scallions)
20 g (¾ oz) coriander
  (cilantro) leaves

DRESSING
2 tablespoons tamari
2 tablespoons maple syrup
2 tablespoons lime juice
1 teaspoon gochujang paste
1 teaspoon cornflour
  (cornstarch)

2: red (bell) pepper
*high in vit C & A
& fibre*

SERVES: 2 PREP: 5 minutes
COOK: 25 minutes

7: spring onion (scallion)
*source of vit C,
calcium & magnesium*

3: purple sprouting broccoli
*source of vit C
& A & folate*

8: lime
high in vit C

4: carrot
*high in vit K, fibre
& beta-carotene*

9: coriander (cilantro)
*source of vit C,
folate & potassium*

METHOD:

1 Cook the barley in a saucepan of water for 25 minutes, or according to the pack instructions. **2** Whisk the dressing ingredients together. **3** Heat the sesame oil in a large frying pan or wok over a high heat, add the sliced red pepper, broccoli, large pieces sliced in half lengthways, carrots, cut into batons, grated garlic, grated ginger and sliced spring onions and fry, stirring, for 5–8 minutes until starting to colour. **4** Add the barley and stir through. **5** Add the dressing and stir to coat. Sprinkle with the coriander and serve.

CHICKEN RICE SALAD

There is an amazing amount of plant goodness in this griddled chicken seasonal winter citrus salad.

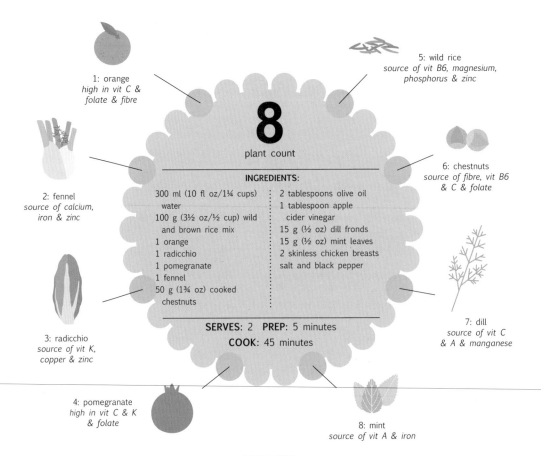

1: orange
high in vit C & folate & fibre

5: wild rice
source of vit B6, magnesium, phosphorus & zinc

2: fennel
source of calcium, iron & zinc

6: chestnuts
source of fibre, vit B6 & C & folate

3: radicchio
source of vit K, copper & zinc

7: dill
source of vit C & A & manganese

4: pomegranate
high in vit C & K & folate

8: mint
source of vit A & iron

8
plant count

INGREDIENTS:

300 ml (10 fl oz/1¼ cups) water
100 g (3½ oz/½ cup) wild and brown rice mix
1 orange
1 radicchio
1 pomegranate
1 fennel
50 g (1¾ oz) cooked chestnuts

2 tablespoons olive oil
1 tablespoon apple cider vinegar
15 g (½ oz) dill fronds
15 g (½ oz) mint leaves
2 skinless chicken breasts
salt and black pepper

SERVES: 2   PREP: 5 minutes
COOK: 45 minutes

METHOD:

1 Pour the 300 ml (10 fl oz/1¼ cups) water into a large saucepan, add the wild rice and bring to the boil. Reduce the heat and simmer for 40–45 minutes until cooked. **2** Peel the orange, cut out each segment, then add to a large bowl. **3** Cut the end off the radicchio, tear the leaves and add to the bowl. **4** Halve the pomegranate, remove the seeds and add to the bowl. **5** Add the thinly sliced fennel, chopped chestnuts, 1 tablespoon oil, vinegar and herbs. **6** Heat a griddle or frying pan. **7** Rub the rest of oil onto the chicken, season and fry the chicken on either side until cooked through. Keep warm. **8** Drain the cooked rice and rinse under cold water. Add to the bowl and stir well. Serve with the sliced chicken.

SPRING STEW

A bowl of greenness marking the months of spring – fresh, slightly sweet and several pops of goodness.

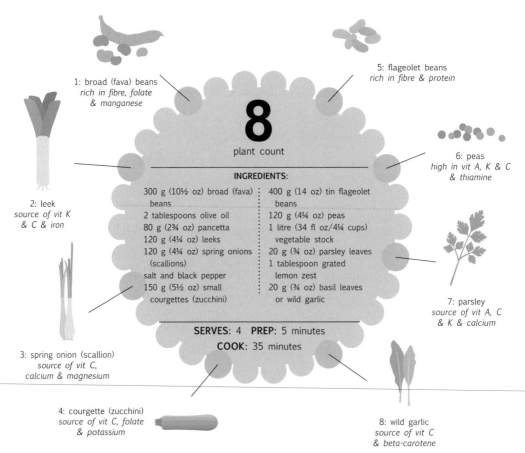

1: broad (fava) beans
rich in fibre, folate & manganese

5: flageolet beans
rich in fibre & protein

8
plant count

6: peas
high in vit A, K & C & thiamine

2: leek
source of vit K & C & iron

INGREDIENTS:

300 g (10½ oz) broad (fava) beans
2 tablespoons olive oil
80 g (2¾ oz) pancetta
120 g (4¼ oz) leeks
120 g (4¼ oz) spring onions (scallions)
salt and black pepper
150 g (5½ oz) small courgettes (zucchini)

400 g (14 oz) tin flageolet beans
120 g (4¼ oz) peas
1 litre (34 fl oz/4¼ cups) vegetable stock
20 g (¾ oz) parsley leaves
1 tablespoon grated lemon zest
20 g (¾ oz) basil leaves or wild garlic

7: parsley
source of vit A, C & K & calcium

SERVES: 4   PREP: 5 minutes
COOK: 35 minutes

3: spring onion (scallion)
source of vit C, calcium & magnesium

4: courgette (zucchini)
source of vit C, folate & potassium

8: wild garlic
source of vit C & beta-carotene

METHOD:

1 Bring a large saucepan of water to the boil, add the podded broad beans and boil for 4–5 minutes. Drain. **2** Heat the oil in a frying pan, add the chopped pancetta and fry for 4–5 minutes until crispy. **3** Add the sliced leeks, sliced spring onions and season. Cover with a lid and sweat for 10–15 minutes. **4** Uncover, add the courgettes, roughly chopped into small pieces, and cook, without the lid, for another 3 minutes. **5** Add the drained flageolet beans, peas and stock. Reduce the heat and simmer for a further 5 minutes. **6** Turn off the heat and stir in the broad beans. Top with the parsley and lemon zest and serve with torn basil or chopped wild garlic.

FALAFEL BOWL

A great lunch option, this is packed full of textures, along with a colourful array of vegetables.

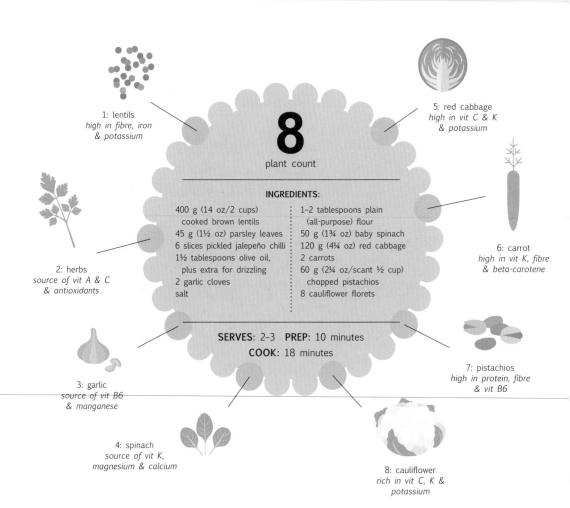

8

plant count

1: lentils
*high in fibre, iron
& potassium*

5: red cabbage
*high in vit C & K
& potassium*

2: herbs
*source of vit A & C
& antioxidants*

6: carrot
*high in vit K, fibre
& beta-carotene*

3: garlic
*source of vit B6
& manganese*

7: pistachios
*high in protein, fibre
& vit B6*

4: spinach
*source of vit K,
magnesium & calcium*

8: cauliflower
*rich in vit C, K &
potassium*

INGREDIENTS:

400 g (14 oz/2 cups)
  cooked brown lentils
45 g (1½ oz) parsley leaves
6 slices pickled jalepeño chilli
1½ tablespoons olive oil,
  plus extra for drizzling
2 garlic cloves
salt

1–2 tablespoons plain
  (all-purpose) flour
50 g (1¾ oz) baby spinach
120 g (4¼ oz) red cabbage
2 carrots
60 g (2¼ oz/scant ½ cup)
  chopped pistachios
8 cauliflower florets

SERVES: 2–3 **PREP:** 10 minutes
COOK: 18 minutes

METHOD:

1 Preheat the oven to 180°C (350°F). **2** Add the lentils, parsley, jalapeño, oil, garlic and 1 teaspoon salt to a food processor and blitz until the mixture sticks together when you press it. **3** Stir in the flour until it's just dry enough to handle, then form the mixture into nine patties. **4** Bake in the oven for 18 minutes. **5** Arrange the spinach, sliced cabbage, carrots, shaved into ribbons, pistachios and steamed cauliflower in a bowl. Add 4–5 falafel to each serving and drizzle with oil.

ONE POT

Simple suppers using just one pot are easy to create, and flexible when it comes to ingredients. Try some of the tasty pasta classics with a slight twist of an extra plant or two. There are also delicious rice dishes mixing up wholegrains and using a variety of beans. This chapter increases your plant count, in a subtle way, making it a game changer.

PANCAKES

Try these pancakes at the weekend. If you need to make more, just double the recipe. Use sunflower or sesame seeds instead of pumpkin seeds, if liked.

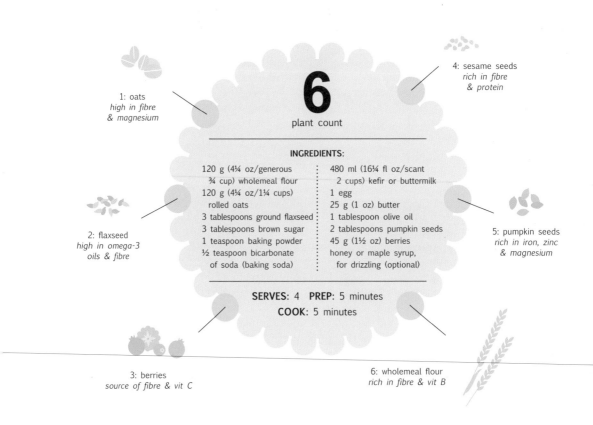

1: oats
*high in fibre
& magnesium*

4: sesame seeds
*rich in fibre
& protein*

6

plant count

2: flaxseed
*high in omega-3
oils & fibre*

5: pumpkin seeds
*rich in iron, zinc
& magnesium*

INGREDIENTS:

120 g (4¼ oz/generous ¾ cup) wholemeal flour	480 ml (16¼ fl oz/scant 2 cups) kefir or buttermilk
120 g (4¼ oz/1¼ cups) rolled oats	1 egg
3 tablespoons ground flaxseed	25 g (1 oz) butter
3 tablespoons brown sugar	1 tablespoon olive oil
1 teaspoon baking powder	2 tablespoons pumpkin seeds
½ teaspoon bicarbonate of soda (baking soda)	45 g (1½ oz) berries honey or maple syrup, for drizzling (optional)

SERVES: 4 PREP: 5 minutes
COOK: 5 minutes

3: berries
source of fibre & vit C

6: wholemeal flour
rich in fibre & vit B

METHOD:

1 Combine the flour, oats, flaxseed, sugar, baking powder and bicarbonate of soda in a large bowl. **2** Pour in the kefir and beaten egg and stir well. **3** Heat a large frying pan with half the butter and oil. **4** Add 2 large tablespoons of batter for one pancake and cook until the bubbles form on top and the edges look dry.
5 Sprinkle with the seeds, flip over and cook until golden on other side. **6** Remove and repeat to make three more pancakes. Serve with berries and honey, if liked.

SHAKSHUKA

This egg-based breakfast, lunch or dinner is filled to the brim with greenness.
Increase your plant count goodness right here.

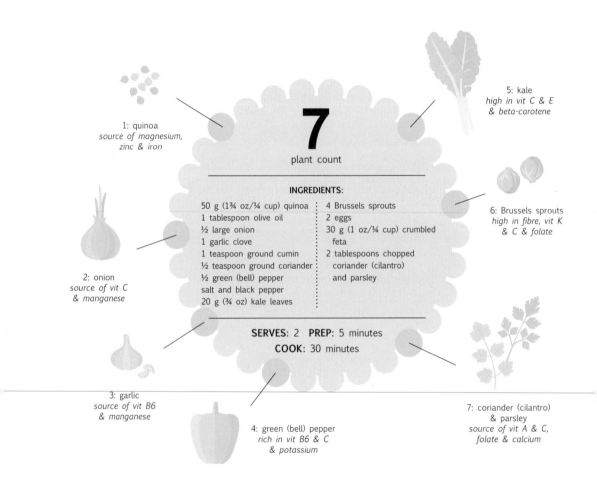

7

plant count

5: kale
*high in vit C & E
& beta-carotene*

1: quinoa
*source of magnesium,
zinc & iron*

INGREDIENTS:

50 g (1¾ oz/¼ cup) quinoa
1 tablespoon olive oil
½ large onion
1 garlic clove
1 teaspoon ground cumin
½ teaspoon ground coriander
½ green (bell) pepper
salt and black pepper
20 g (¾ oz) kale leaves

4 Brussels sprouts
2 eggs
30 g (1 oz/¼ cup) crumbled
  feta
2 tablespoons chopped
  coriander (cilantro)
  and parsley

6: Brussels sprouts
*high in fibre, vit K
& C & folate*

SERVES: 2 **PREP:** 5 minutes
COOK: 30 minutes

2: onion
*source of vit C
& manganese*

3: garlic
*source of vit B6
& manganese*

4: green (bell) pepper
*rich in vit B6 & C
& potassium*

7: coriander (cilantro)
& parsley
*source of vit A & C,
folate & calcium*

METHOD:

1 Cook the quinoa according to the pack instructions. **2** Heat the oil in a frying pan and cook the sliced onion and grated garlic until transluscent. **3** Add the spices and sliced green pepper, season and cook for 3 minutes. **4** Add the shredded kale and Brussels sprouts and cook for 6–8 minutes until cooked down a little. **5** Stir through the quinoa, then create two wells for the eggs. Season and crack an egg into each well. **6** Lay a lid or baking tray (pan) over the top and cook until the top of the eggs are cooked. **7** Sprinkle with the feta and herbs.

SCRAMBLED EGG

This Puttanesca-style scramble has all the sharp and salty flavours that go so well with the creamy eggs. No eggs? Try it with tofu.

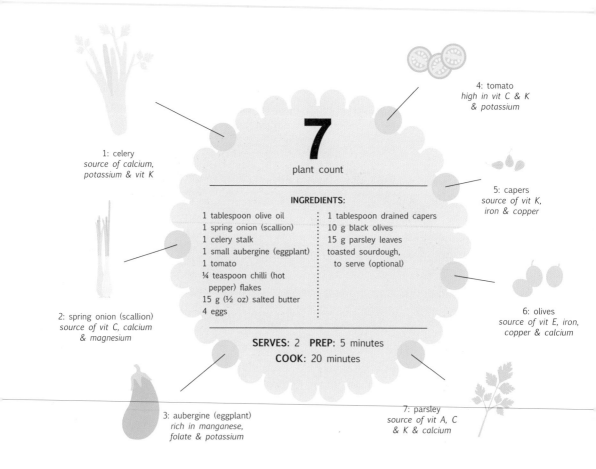

1: celery
source of calcium, potassium & vit K

2: spring onion (scallion)
source of vit C, calcium & magnesium

3: aubergine (eggplant)
rich in manganese, folate & potassium

4: tomato
high in vit C & K & potassium

5: capers
source of vit K, iron & copper

6: olives
source of vit E, iron, copper & calcium

7: parsley
source of vit A, C & K & calcium

7
plant count

INGREDIENTS:

1 tablespoon olive oil
1 spring onion (scallion)
1 celery stalk
1 small aubergine (eggplant)
1 tomato
¼ teaspoon chilli (hot pepper) flakes
15 g (½ oz) salted butter
4 eggs

1 tablespoon drained capers
10 g black olives
15 g parsley leaves
toasted sourdough, to serve (optional)

SERVES: 2 **PREP:** 5 minutes
COOK: 20 minutes

METHOD:

1 Heat the oil in a large frying pan and cook the sliced spring onion and celery for 2 minutes. **2** Add the peeled and diced aubergine and cook for 3 minutes. **3** Add the chopped tomato and chilli flakes and cook for 3 minutes. **4** Using a spatula, move the ingredients to one side of the pan, add the butter to the other side and melt. **5** Reduce the heat to low, add the beaten eggs and cook, stirring occasionally. **6** Once the eggs are cooked, toss the capers, olives and finely chopped parsley over the vegetables and warm through. **7** Serve the eggs with the vegetables on top and toasted sourdough, if liked.

VEGETABLE FRITTERS

Who doesn't love a fritter? These tasty root veg ones have all the plant goodness you need. They are great served with a plain yoghurt dip, such as raita, and try adding cucumber and beetroot (beet) to it for extra plant points.

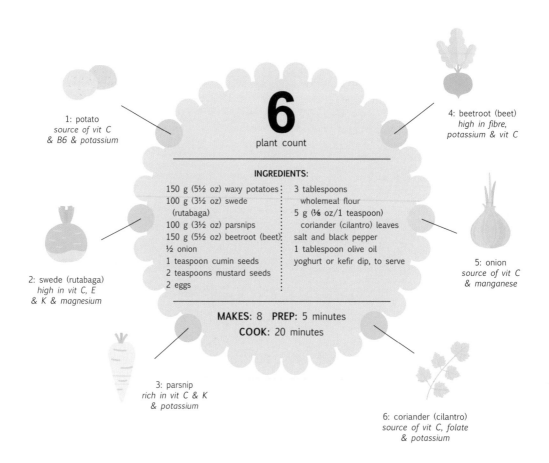

6
plant count

1: potato
*source of vit C
& B6 & potassium*

4: beetroot (beet)
*high in fibre,
potassium & vit C*

2: swede (rutabaga)
*high in vit C, E
& K & magnesium*

5: onion
*source of vit C
& manganese*

3: parsnip
*rich in vit C & K
& potassium*

6: coriander (cilantro)
*source of vit C, folate
& potassium*

INGREDIENTS:

150 g (5½ oz) waxy potatoes
100 g (3½ oz) swede (rutabaga)
100 g (3½ oz) parsnips
150 g (5½ oz) beetroot (beet)
½ onion
1 teaspoon cumin seeds
2 teaspoons mustard seeds
2 eggs

3 tablespoons wholemeal flour
5 g (⅛ oz/1 teaspoon) coriander (cilantro) leaves
salt and black pepper
1 tablespoon olive oil
yoghurt or kefir dip, to serve

MAKES: 8 **PREP:** 5 minutes
COOK: 20 minutes

METHOD:

1 Grate the potatoes, swede, parsnips, beetroot and onion, then add to a large bowl with the cumin, mustard seeds, eggs, flour and chopped coriander. **2** Mix well until combined. Season to taste. **3** Using wet hands, make 8 portions of the mixture. **4** Heat the oil in a large frying pan and cook the fritters in batches for 5 minutes on each side, then drain on paper towels. Serve with yoghurt or kefir dip.

CHILLI CON QUINOA

A tasty soul warming beef chilli, but cooked with squash and quinoa for extra plant goodness. Serve with a flatbread, corn chips and a simple green salad.

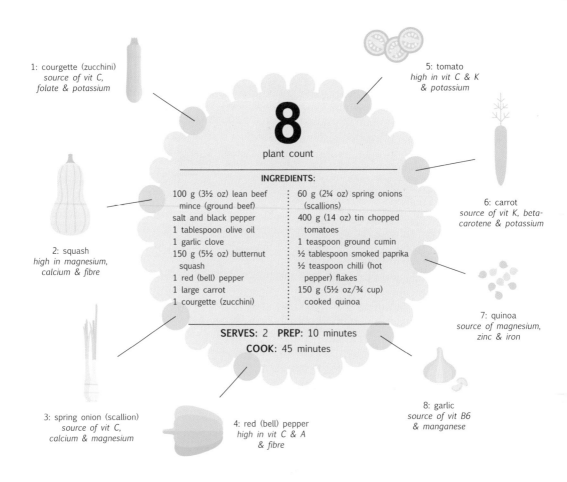

1: courgette (zucchini)
source of vit C, folate & potassium

5: tomato
high in vit C & K & potassium

6: carrot
source of vit K, beta-carotene & potassium

2: squash
high in magnesium, calcium & fibre

7: quinoa
source of magnesium, zinc & iron

3: spring onion (scallion)
source of vit C, calcium & magnesium

4: red (bell) pepper
high in vit C & A & fibre

8: garlic
source of vit B6 & manganese

8
plant count

INGREDIENTS:

100 g (3½ oz) lean beef mince (ground beef)
salt and black pepper
1 tablespoon olive oil
1 garlic clove
150 g (5½ oz) butternut squash
1 red (bell) pepper
1 large carrot
1 courgette (zucchini)

60 g (2¼ oz) spring onions (scallions)
400 g (14 oz) tin chopped tomatoes
1 teaspoon ground cumin
½ tablespoon smoked paprika
½ teaspoon chilli (hot pepper) flakes
150 g (5½ oz/¾ cup) cooked quinoa

SERVES: 2 PREP: 10 minutes
COOK: 45 minutes

METHOD:

1 Season the beef with salt and pepper. **2** Heat the oil in a large frying pan and cook the beef over a medium-high heat until browned all over. Set aside. **3** Add the grated garlic, peeled and diced squash, diced red pepper, diced carrot and courgette to the pan and cook until just softened. **4** Add the sliced spring onions, chopped tomatoes, cooked beef, spices and 2 tablespoons water. Bring to the boil, cover and reduce the heat. **5** Simmer for 15 minutes, or until the vegetables are soft. Season to taste. **6** Add the quinoa and cook for another 5 minutes.

MAC 'N' CHEESE

Packed full of green veg, this mac 'n' cheese could become a firm family favourite.
Serve with a mixed green salad to increase your plant points.

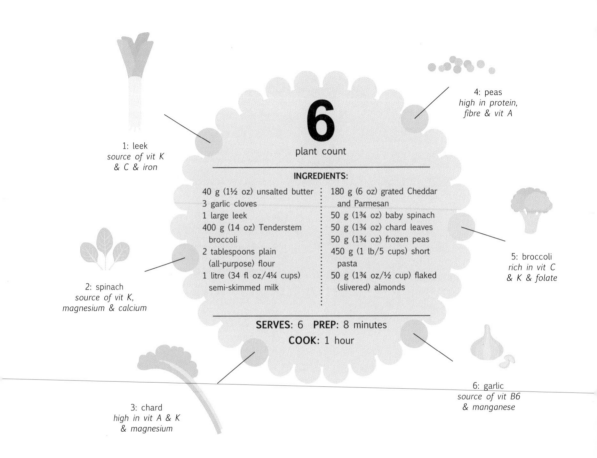

6

plant count

1: leek
*source of vit K
& C & iron*

2: spinach
*source of vit K,
magnesium & calcium*

3: chard
*high in vit A & K
& magnesium*

4: peas
*high in protein,
fibre & vit A*

5: broccoli
*rich in vit C
& K & folate*

6: garlic
*source of vit B6
& manganese*

INGREDIENTS:

40 g (1½ oz) unsalted butter
3 garlic cloves
1 large leek
400 g (14 oz) Tenderstem broccoli
2 tablespoons plain (all-purpose) flour
1 litre (34 fl oz/4¼ cups) semi-skimmed milk

180 g (6 oz) grated Cheddar and Parmesan
50 g (1¾ oz) baby spinach
50 g (1¾ oz) chard leaves
50 g (1¾ oz) frozen peas
450 g (1 lb/5 cups) short pasta
50 g (1¾ oz/½ cup) flaked (slivered) almonds

SERVES: 6   **PREP:** 8 minutes
COOK: 1 hour

METHOD:

1 Preheat the oven to 180°C (350°F). **2** Melt the butter in a large saucepan and cook the sliced garlic, chopped leek and broccoli until softened. **3** Stir in the flour, then slowly add the milk. Simmer until thickened. **4** Add the grated cheese, spinach, chard and thawed peas and cook for 2 minutes. **5** Blitz in a blender until smooth, stir in the pasta, blanched for 5 minutes, then pour into a 25 x 35 cm (10 x 14 in) baking dish. Sprinkle with the flaked almonds. **6** Bake for 30 minutes.

MINESTRONE PASTA

This soup can be changed depending on the season. Here, is a recipe for spring, but swap some of the green vegetables for winter veg like cabbage and carrots, and the beans for heavier ones like borlotti.

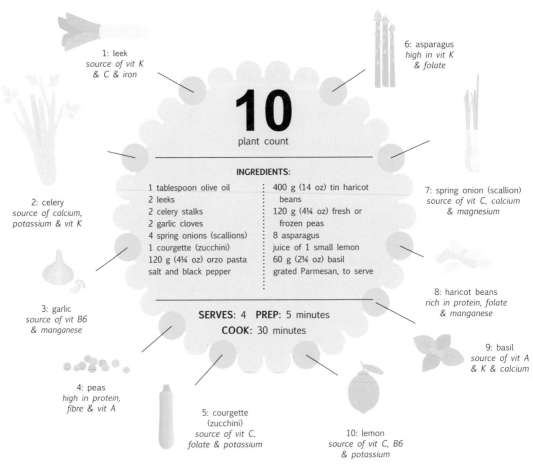

1: leek
source of vit K & C & iron

6: asparagus
high in vit K & folate

10
plant count

INGREDIENTS:

1 tablespoon olive oil
2 leeks
2 celery stalks
2 garlic cloves
4 spring onions (scallions)
1 courgette (zucchini)
120 g (4¼ oz) orzo pasta
salt and black pepper

400 g (14 oz) tin haricot beans
120 g (4¼ oz) fresh or frozen peas
8 asparagus
juice of 1 small lemon
60 g (2¼ oz) basil
grated Parmesan, to serve

SERVES: 4 PREP: 5 minutes
COOK: 30 minutes

2: celery
source of calcium, potassium & vit K

7: spring onion (scallion)
source of vit C, calcium & magnesium

3: garlic
source of vit B6 & manganese

8: haricot beans
rich in protein, folate & manganese

9: basil
source of vit A & K & calcium

4: peas
high in protein, fibre & vit A

5: courgette (zucchini)
source of vit C, folate & potassium

10: lemon
source of vit C, B6 & potassium

METHOD:

1 Heat the oil in a large saucepan and fry the chopped leeks and diced celery until softened. **2** Add the grated garlic, sliced spring onions and diced courgette and cook for 3 minutes. **3** Add 1 litre (34 fl oz/4¼ cups) water, then add the orzo. Bring to the boil. Season and simmer for 10 minutes. **4** Add the drained beans, peas and sliced asparagus and cook for 4 minutes, or until the asparagus are just cooked. **5** Take off the heat, squeeze over the lemon juice and add the chopped basil. Stir and serve with cheese.

TOMATO SAUCE

This super plant-boost recipe works with so many meals. Try it blitzed on top of pizza or in a ragu, on lasagne or over meatballs. Make a big batch and freeze it.

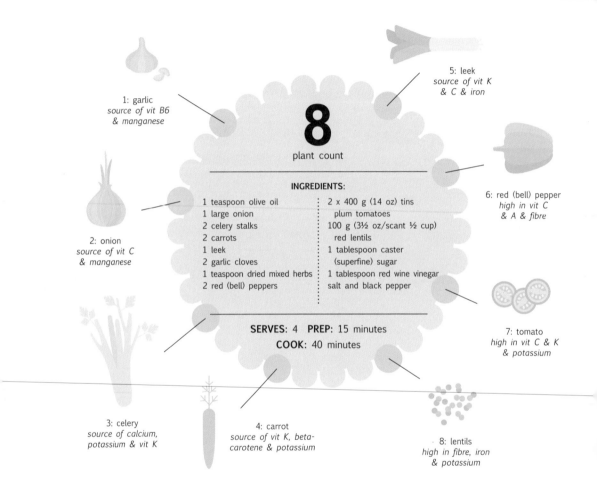

1: garlic
*source of vit B6
& manganese*

2: onion
*source of vit C
& manganese*

3: celery
*source of calcium,
potassium & vit K*

4: carrot
*source of vit K, beta-
carotene & potassium*

5: leek
*source of vit K
& C & iron*

6: red (bell) pepper
*high in vit C
& A & fibre*

7: tomato
*high in vit C & K
& potassium*

8: lentils
*high in fibre, iron
& potassium*

8

plant count

INGREDIENTS:

1 teaspoon olive oil
1 large onion
2 celery stalks
2 carrots
1 leek
2 garlic cloves
1 teaspoon dried mixed herbs
2 red (bell) peppers

2 x 400 g (14 oz) tins
   plum tomatoes
100 g (3½ oz/scant ½ cup)
   red lentils
1 tablespoon caster
   (superfine) sugar
1 tablespoon red wine vinegar
salt and black pepper

SERVES: 4 PREP: 15 minutes
COOK: 40 minutes

METHOD:

1 Heat the oil in a large saucepan and cook the chopped onion, celery, carrots and leek gently until soft. **2** Add the grated garlic, dried herbs and chopped peppers and cook for 10 minutes. **3** Add the tomatoes, lentils, sugar and vinegar, season and simmer for 20 minutes, stirring occasionally. **4** Once the lentils are soft, season again to taste. Store in the refrigerator for five days or freeze for up to three months.

SPICED COD

This tasty supper is so simple, packed full of plants and big on flavour. It uses green pesto, but you can use red pesto too, if you prefer.

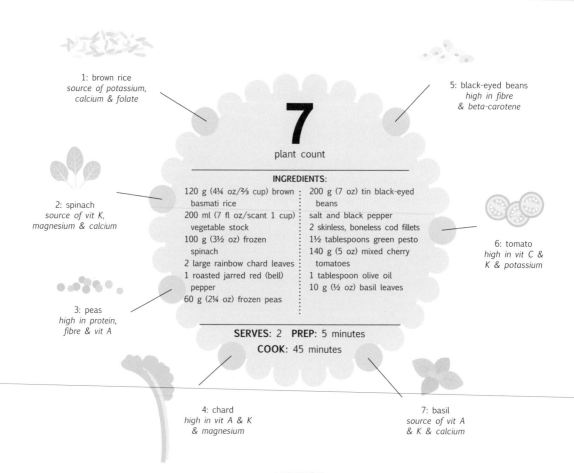

1: brown rice
source of potassium, calcium & folate

5: black-eyed beans
high in fibre & beta-carotene

7
plant count

2: spinach
source of vit K, magnesium & calcium

6: tomato
high in vit C & K & potassium

3: peas
high in protein, fibre & vit A

INGREDIENTS:

120 g (4¼ oz/⅔ cup) brown basmati rice
200 ml (7 fl oz/scant 1 cup) vegetable stock
100 g (3½ oz) frozen spinach
2 large rainbow chard leaves
1 roasted jarred red (bell) pepper
60 g (2¼ oz) frozen peas

200 g (7 oz) tin black-eyed beans
salt and black pepper
2 skinless, boneless cod fillets
1½ tablespoons green pesto
140 g (5 oz) mixed cherry tomatoes
1 tablespoon olive oil
10 g (½ oz) basil leaves

SERVES: 2 PREP: 5 minutes
COOK: 45 minutes

4: chard
high in vit A & K & magnesium

7: basil
source of vit A & K & calcium

METHOD:

1 Add the rice to a wide ovenproof saucepan, add the stock and bring to the boil.
2 Reduce the heat, cover and simmer for 20–25 minutes until the rice is tender and the liquid has been absorbed. **3** Meanwhile, preheat the oven to 220°C (425°F).
4 Stir the thawed spinach, chard, stalks removed, sliced red peppers, peas and drained beans through the rice. **5** Season the fish and arrange over the rice.
6 Brush the fish with the pesto, scatter with the tomatoes and drizzle with the oil.
7 Bake for 12–15 minutes, uncovered, until the fish is cooked. Sprinkle with torn basil.

TACOS

Omit the pork for a vegetarian or vegan option. These delicious tacos fill you up with a great variety of plants. Use corn instead of wheat tortilla wraps for more plant points.

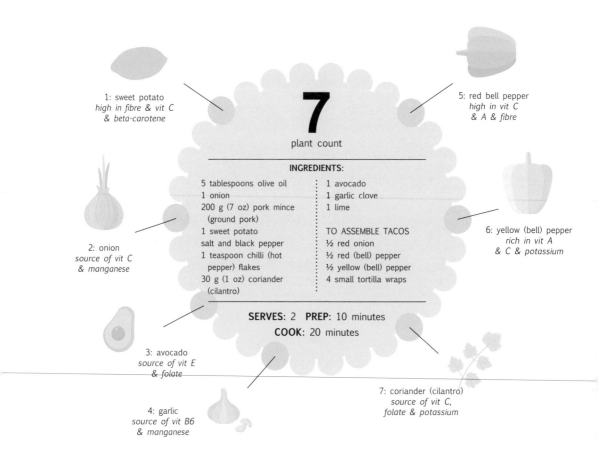

7

plant count

1: sweet potato
*high in fibre & vit C
& beta-carotene*

2: onion
*source of vit C
& manganese*

3: avocado
*source of vit E
& folate*

4: garlic
*source of vit B6
& manganese*

5: red bell pepper
*high in vit C
& A & fibre*

6: yellow (bell) pepper
*rich in vit A
& C & potassium*

7: coriander (cilantro)
*source of vit C,
folate & potassium*

INGREDIENTS:

5 tablespoons olive oil	1 avocado
1 onion	1 garlic clove
200 g (7 oz) pork mince	1 lime
(ground pork)	
1 sweet potato	TO ASSEMBLE TACOS
salt and black pepper	½ red onion
1 teaspoon chilli (hot	½ red (bell) pepper
pepper) flakes	½ yellow (bell) pepper
30 g (1 oz) coriander	4 small tortilla wraps
(cilantro)	

SERVES: 2 **PREP:** 10 minutes
COOK: 20 minutes

METHOD:

1 Heat 1 tablespoon of the oil in a frying pan and cook the chopped onion until translucent. **2** Add the pork and sweet potato, cut into batons, and cook over a high heat for 5 minutes, or until the pork has some colour. **3** Season and add the chilli flakes, then cook for 2 minutes. Set aside. **4** Blitz the coriander, peeled and stoned avocado, garlic, lime juice and remaining oil to make a dressing. **5** To assemble the tacos, slice the onion and peppers and warm the tortilla wraps. Layer the wraps with the dressing, pork, sweet potato and vegetables.

CHICKEN CURRY

A warming coconut curry with flavours of perky ginger, served with brown rice or noodles. Make sure the chicken is skinless and boneless.

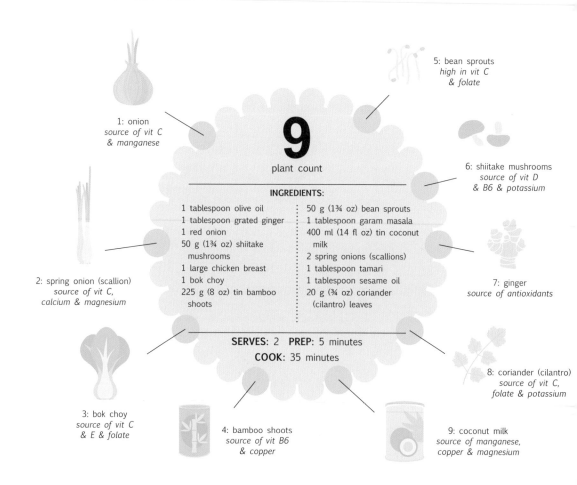

1: onion
*source of vit C
& manganese*

2: spring onion (scallion)
*source of vit C,
calcium & magnesium*

3: bok choy
*source of vit C
& E & folate*

4: bamboo shoots
*source of vit B6
& copper*

5: bean sprouts
*high in vit C
& folate*

6: shiitake mushrooms
*source of vit D
& B6 & potassium*

7: ginger
source of antioxidants

8: coriander (cilantro)
*source of vit C,
folate & potassium*

9: coconut milk
*source of manganese,
copper & magnesium*

9
plant count

INGREDIENTS:

1 tablespoon olive oil
1 tablespoon grated ginger
1 red onion
50 g (1¾ oz) shiitake
   mushrooms
1 large chicken breast
1 bok choy
225 g (8 oz) tin bamboo
   shoots

50 g (1¾ oz) bean sprouts
1 tablespoon garam masala
400 ml (14 fl oz) tin coconut
   milk
2 spring onions (scallions)
1 tablespoon tamari
1 tablespoon sesame oil
20 g (¾ oz) coriander
   (cilantro) leaves

SERVES: 2 **PREP:** 5 minutes
COOK: 35 minutes

METHOD:

1 Heat the olive oil in a large frying pan and fry the ginger and sliced red onion for 2 minutes. **2** Add the shiitake mushrooms and fry for 4 minutes. **3** Add the chicken, cut into bite-sized pieces, quartered bok choy, drained and rinsed bamboo shoots, rinsed sprouts and garam masala and stir. **4** After 1 minute, add the coconut milk and thinly sliced spring onions and cook until the chicken is tender. **5** Drizzle with tamari and sesame oil, then sprinkle with the chopped coriander.

RAGU

This deep earthy dish is delicious over brown rice, stirred through pasta as a sauce, or even with courgetti (zucchini noodles) adding for an extra plant point.

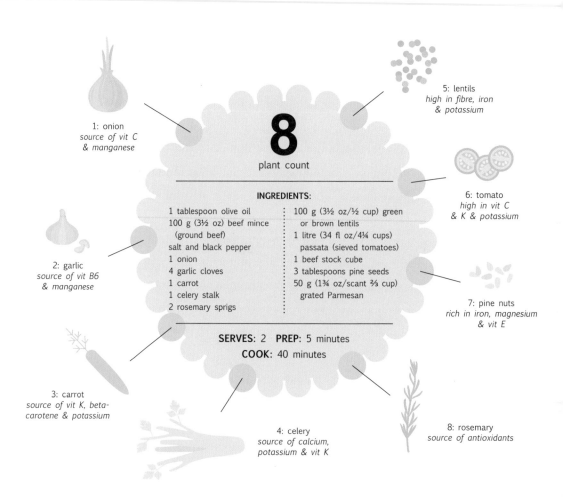

8

plant count

1: onion
*source of vit C
& manganese*

2: garlic
*source of vit B6
& manganese*

3: carrot
*source of vit K, beta-
carotene & potassium*

4: celery
*source of calcium,
potassium & vit K*

5: lentils
*high in fibre, iron
& potassium*

6: tomato
*high in vit C
& K & potassium*

7: pine nuts
*rich in iron, magnesium
& vit E*

8: rosemary
source of antioxidants

INGREDIENTS:

1 tablespoon olive oil	100 g (3½ oz/½ cup) green
100 g (3½ oz) beef mince	or brown lentils
(ground beef)	1 litre (34 fl oz/4¼ cups)
salt and black pepper	passata (sieved tomatoes)
1 onion	1 beef stock cube
4 garlic cloves	3 tablespoons pine seeds
1 carrot	50 g (1¾ oz/scant ⅔ cup)
1 celery stalk	grated Parmesan
2 rosemary sprigs	

SERVES: 2 **PREP:** 5 minutes
COOK: 40 minutes

METHOD:

1 Heat the oil in a large frying pan, add the mince, season and fry, stirring, until there is no pink showing. Tip the beef out and set aside. **2** Add the chopped onion and grated garlic to the pan and fry until translucent. **3** Add the chopped carrot and celery and fry for 7 minutes. **4** Add the rosemary and lentils and stir for 2 minutes. **5** Add the passata and stock cube. **6** Return the mince to the pan and cover. Simmer over a low heat for 30 minutes. **7** Mix the pine nuts with the grated Parmesan. Serve the ragu sprinkled with the pine nut mixture.

KIMCHI RICE

This is a great way to use up any leftover rice with the great addition of kimchi, a fantastic Korean staple of fermented cabbage and vegetables.

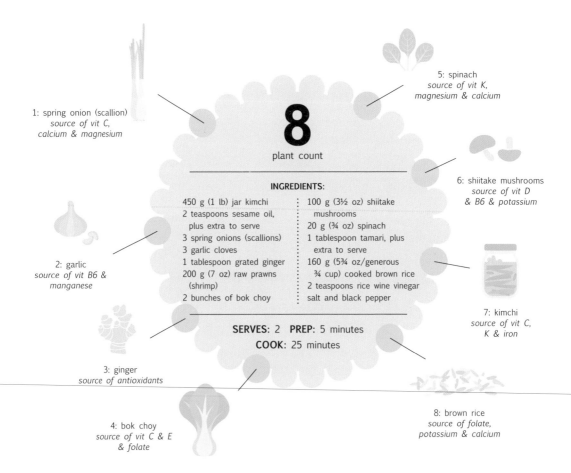

1: spring onion (scallion)
*source of vit C,
calcium & magnesium*

5: spinach
*source of vit K,
magnesium & calcium*

8
plant count

6: shiitake mushrooms
*source of vit D
& B6 & potassium*

2: garlic
*source of vit B6 &
manganese*

INGREDIENTS:

450 g (1 lb) jar kimchi	100 g (3½ oz) shiitake
2 teaspoons sesame oil,	mushrooms
plus extra to serve	20 g (¾ oz) spinach
3 spring onions (scallions)	1 tablespoon tamari, plus
3 garlic cloves	extra to serve
1 tablespoon grated ginger	160 g (5¾ oz/generous
200 g (7 oz) raw prawns	¾ cup) cooked brown rice
(shrimp)	2 teaspoons rice wine vinegar
2 bunches of bok choy	salt and black pepper

SERVES: 2 **PREP:** 5 minutes
COOK: 25 minutes

7: kimchi
*source of vit C,
K & iron*

3: ginger
source of antioxidants

4: bok choy
*source of vit C & E
& folate*

8: brown rice
*source of folate,
potassium & calcium*

METHOD:

1 Drain the kimchi, reserving the liquid, and chop into bite-sized pieces. Set aside.
2 Heat the sesame oil in a large frying pan and fry the sliced spring onions for
2–3 minutes. **3** Stir in the grated garlic and ginger and cook for 1 minute. **4** Add
the shelled prawns, thinly sliced bok choy, thinly sliced mushrooms and spinach
and cook for 2–3 minutes until the prawns have turned pink. **5** Add the kimchi and
tamari and cook until just heated through. **6** Add the rice, 1 tablespoon of the
reserved kimchi brine and the vinegar and cook for 3–4 minutes stirring frequently.
7 Season and add more tamari and sesame oil.

BEEF MASALA

A plant-boosting curry using lentils and cashews to give it a creamy consistency.
Add more chilli powder if you like it hot! Serve with rice or flatbread.

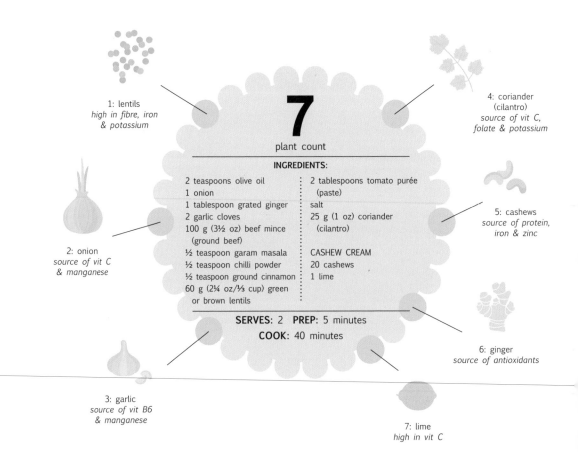

1: lentils
*high in fibre, iron
& potassium*

2: onion
*source of vit C
& manganese*

3: garlic
*source of vit B6
& manganese*

4: coriander
(cilantro)
*source of vit C,
folate & potassium*

5: cashews
*source of protein,
iron & zinc*

6: ginger
source of antioxidants

7: lime
high in vit C

7
plant count

INGREDIENTS:

2 teaspoons olive oil
1 onion
1 tablespoon grated ginger
2 garlic cloves
100 g (3½ oz) beef mince
 (ground beef)
½ teaspoon garam masala
½ teaspoon chilli powder
½ teaspoon ground cinnamon
60 g (2¼ oz/⅓ cup) green
 or brown lentils

2 tablespoons tomato purée
 (paste)
salt
25 g (1 oz) coriander
 (cilantro)

CASHEW CREAM
20 cashews
1 lime

SERVES: 2 **PREP:** 5 minutes
COOK: 40 minutes

METHOD:

1 Heat the oil in a frying pan over a medium-low heat and cook the chopped onion for 7 minutes. **2** Add the ginger and grated garlic and cook for 2–3 minutes. **3** Add the beef and cook all the way through. **4** Stir in the spices, add the lentils, tomato purée and 300 ml (10 fl oz/1¼ cups) water. Bring to a simmer, adding a little more water to loosen, if needed. Cover and cook until the lentils are tender. **5** For the cashew cream, blitz the nuts, lime juice and 100 ml (3½ fl oz/scant ½ cup) warm water in a blender until smooth. **6** Stir the cashew cream into the curry, season to taste with salt and sprinkle with the coriander.

RISOTTO

A warming bowl of goodness, ready from start to finish in 30 minutes.
Use ceps instead of chestnut mushrooms, if you prefer.

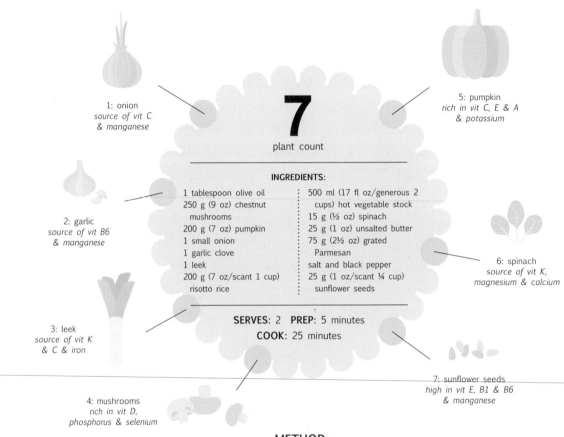

1: onion
source of vit C & manganese

2: garlic
source of vit B6 & manganese

3: leek
source of vit K & C & iron

4: mushrooms
rich in vit D, phosphorus & selenium

5: pumpkin
rich in vit C, E & A & potassium

6: spinach
source of vit K, magnesium & calcium

7: sunflower seeds
high in vit E, B1 & B6 & manganese

7
plant count

INGREDIENTS:

1 tablespoon olive oil
250 g (9 oz) chestnut mushrooms
200 g (7 oz) pumpkin
1 small onion
1 garlic clove
1 leek
200 g (7 oz/scant 1 cup) risotto rice
500 ml (17 fl oz/generous 2 cups) hot vegetable stock
15 g (½ oz) spinach
25 g (1 oz) unsalted butter
75 g (2½ oz) grated Parmesan
salt and black pepper
25 g (1 oz/scant ¼ cup) sunflower seeds

SERVES: 2 PREP: 5 minutes
COOK: 25 minutes

METHOD:

1 Heat the oil in a saucepan over a high heat and cook the chopped mushrooms and pumpkin, cut into cubes for 3 minutes. Set aside. **2** Add the pan to a medium-low heat and cook the chopped onion and grated garlic until softened. **3** Add the chopped leek and cook until softened. **4** Add the rice and fry for 1 minute stirring. **5** Add the hot stock, a ladleful at a time, stirring until the liquid is absorbed. **6** After 10 minutes, stir the mushrooms and pumpkin into the pan. Add the stock for another 5 minutes. **7** Once the rice is cooked, add the spinach, butter, half the Parmesan and season. Cover and turn off the heat. **8** Mix the remaining Parmesan with the toasted, chopped seeds. **9** Serve the risotto, sprinkled with the cheese mix.

BURGER

These spiced lamb burgers are packed full of flavours. Serve with your favourite trimmings and add a few more chillies if you like it hot – it can take it.

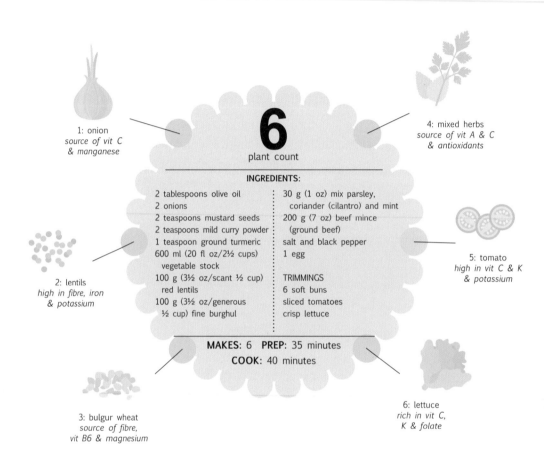

1: onion
source of vit C & manganese

4: mixed herbs
source of vit A & C & antioxidants

6
plant count

INGREDIENTS:

2 tablespoons olive oil
2 onions
2 teaspoons mustard seeds
2 teaspoons mild curry powder
1 teaspoon ground turmeric
600 ml (20 fl oz/2½ cups) vegetable stock
100 g (3½ oz/scant ½ cup) red lentils
100 g (3½ oz/generous ½ cup) fine burghul

30 g (1 oz) mix parsley, coriander (cilantro) and mint
200 g (7 oz) beef mince (ground beef)
salt and black pepper
1 egg

TRIMMINGS
6 soft buns
sliced tomatoes
crisp lettuce

MAKES: 6 **PREP:** 35 minutes
COOK: 40 minutes

2: lentils
high in fibre, iron & potassium

5: tomato
high in vit C & K & potassium

3: bulgur wheat
source of fibre, vit B6 & magnesium

6: lettuce
rich in vit C, K & folate

METHOD:

1 Heat half the oil in a large frying pan over a medium heat and cook the finely chopped onions for 10 minutes, stirring frequently, until soft. **2** Add the spices and fry for 3–4 minutes. **3** Add the stock and lentils and bring to the boil. Cook for 10–15 minutes until the lentils are soft. **4** Stir in the burghul, turn off the heat, cover and cool. **5** Add the finely chopped herbs and beef mince to a large bowl and season. **6** Add the contents of the pan to the bowl, add the egg and mix together with your hands. Form the mixture into six large patties and chill for 30 minutes. **7** Fry the patties in a pan for 4 minutes on each side until golden. Serve in warmed buns with the trimmings.

CHICKEN STIR-FRY

Stir-fries are a great way of increasing your plant count. It is also super quick and very simple to make. Serve with your favourite noodles or rice. Make sure the chicken is skinless and boneless.

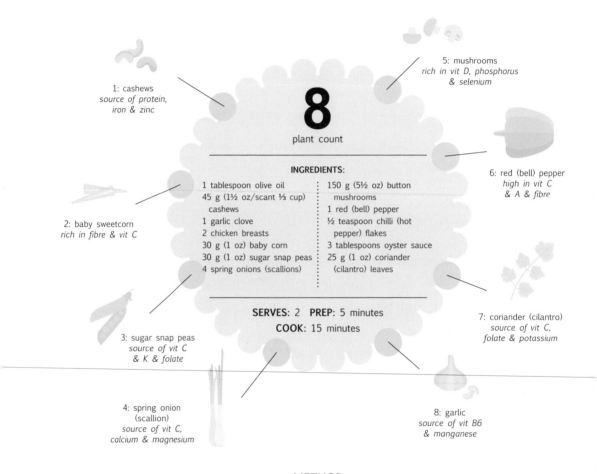

5: mushrooms
*rich in vit D, phosphorus
& selenium*

1: cashews
*source of protein,
iron & zinc*

8
plant count

6: red (bell) pepper
*high in vit C
& A & fibre*

INGREDIENTS:

1 tablespoon olive oil
45 g (1½ oz/scant ⅓ cup) cashews
1 garlic clove
2 chicken breasts
30 g (1 oz) baby corn
30 g (1 oz) sugar snap peas
4 spring onions (scallions)

150 g (5½ oz) button mushrooms
1 red (bell) pepper
½ teaspoon chilli (hot pepper) flakes
3 tablespoons oyster sauce
25 g (1 oz) coriander (cilantro) leaves

2: baby sweetcorn
rich in fibre & vit C

SERVES: 2 **PREP:** 5 minutes
COOK: 15 minutes

7: coriander (cilantro)
*source of vit C,
folate & potassium*

3: sugar snap peas
*source of vit C
& K & folate*

4: spring onion
(scallion)
*source of vit C,
calcium & magnesium*

8: garlic
*source of vit B6
& manganese*

METHOD:

1 Heat the oil in a wok or large frying pan over a medium heat and cook the cashews until lightly toasted. Use a slotted spoon to transfer to a bowl. **2** Add the grated garlic to the wok and cook for 1 minute. **3** Increase the heat to high, add the chicken, cut into bite-sized pieces, and cook for 3–4 minutes, stirring until golden. **4** Add the cashews, corn, sliced sugar snap peas, sliced spring onions, mushrooms, sliced red pepper and chilli flakes. Stir and cook for 2 minutes. **5** Pour in the oyster sauce and sprinkle with the chopped coriander.

LAMB MEATBALLS

These Moroccan style meatballs are served with a delicious aubergine (eggplant) salsa. Try it with a flatbread and create your own sandwich with a crisp green salad. Cook the aubergine in an oven preheated to 250°C (480°F) for 40 minutes.

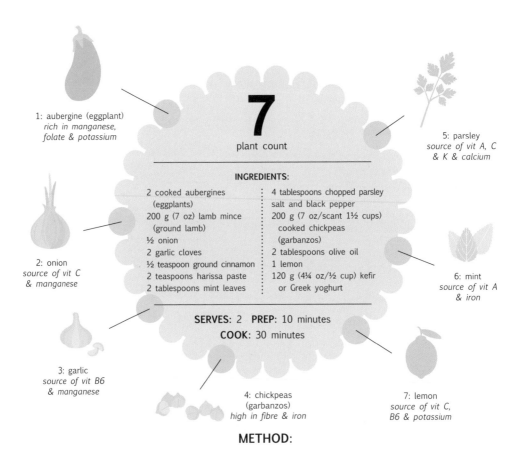

1: aubergine (eggplant)
*rich in manganese,
folate & potassium*

5: parsley
*source of vit A, C
& K & calcium*

7
plant count

INGREDIENTS:

2 cooked aubergines
(eggplants)
200 g (7 oz) lamb mince
(ground lamb)
½ onion
2 garlic cloves
½ teaspoon ground cinnamon
2 teaspoons harissa paste
2 tablespoons mint leaves

4 tablespoons chopped parsley
salt and black pepper
200 g (7 oz/scant 1½ cups)
cooked chickpeas
(garbanzos)
2 tablespoons olive oil
1 lemon
120 g (4¼ oz/½ cup) kefir
or Greek yoghurt

SERVES: 2 **PREP:** 10 minutes
COOK: 30 minutes

2: onion
*source of vit C
& manganese*

6: mint
*source of vit A
& iron*

3: garlic
*source of vit B6
& manganese*

4: chickpeas
(garbanzos)
high in fibre & iron

7: lemon
*source of vit C,
B6 & potassium*

METHOD:

1 Discard the aubergine skins and chop the flesh. **2** Add 80 g (2¾ oz) of the aubergine to a bowl with the lamb, grated onion, grated garlic, cinnamon, 1½ teaspoons harissa, mint, 1 tablespoon parsley and season. Form the mix into six to eight small balls. **3** Stir the remaining harissa through the chickpeas. **4** Heat a frying pan until hot, add a little oil and fry the chickpeas until crispy. Set aside. **5** Add a little more oil to the pan, add the meatballs and fry for 8–10 minutes until browned and cooked through. **6** Squeeze a lemon half over the meatballs. **7** Mix the rest of aubergine with the kefir, 1 tablespoon oil, juice from the other lemon half and season. **8** Serve the meatballs with the salsa, chickpeas and sprinkled with the remaining parsley.

PORK STEW

Try this warming stew cooked in creamy sherry along with a variety of wild mushrooms and pear to help keep your gut happy. It is delicious over rice or with mashed potato.

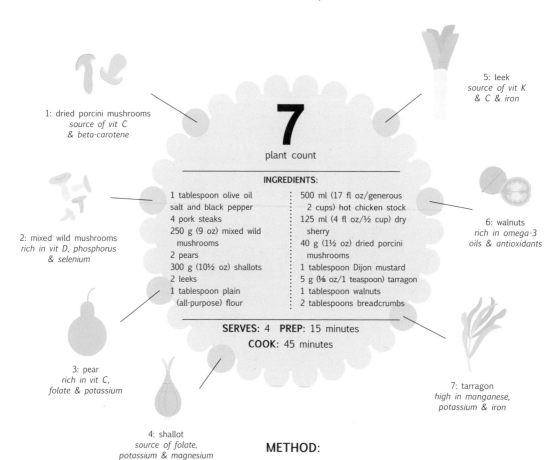

1: dried porcini mushrooms
*source of vit C
& beta-carotene*

2: mixed wild mushrooms
*rich in vit D, phosphorus
& selenium*

3: pear
*rich in vit C,
folate & potassium*

4: shallot
*source of folate,
potassium & magnesium*

5: leek
*source of vit K
& C & iron*

6: walnuts
*rich in omega-3
oils & antioxidants*

7: tarragon
*high in manganese,
potassium & iron*

7
plant count

INGREDIENTS:

1 tablespoon olive oil
salt and black pepper
4 pork steaks
250 g (9 oz) mixed wild
   mushrooms
2 pears
300 g (10½ oz) shallots
2 leeks
1 tablespoon plain
   (all-purpose) flour

500 ml (17 fl oz/generous
   2 cups) hot chicken stock
125 ml (4 fl oz/½ cup) dry
   sherry
40 g (1½ oz) dried porcini
   mushrooms
1 tablespoon Dijon mustard
5 g (⅛ oz/1 teaspoon) tarragon
1 tablespoon walnuts
2 tablespoons breadcrumbs

SERVES: 4 **PREP:** 15 minutes
COOK: 45 minutes

METHOD:

1 Heat the oil in a saucepan. **2** Season the pork, cut into bite-sized chunks, then brown, a few pieces at a time, transferring to a bowl. **3** Fry the chopped mixed mushrooms in the pan until golden. Set aside. **4** Fry the pears, cored and cut into thin wedges, in the pan until golden. Set aside. **5** Cook the shallots and sliced leeks in the pan until soft. **6** Dust the pork in flour, add to the pan, then add 100 ml (3½ fl oz/scant ½ cup) stock. Stir, slowly adding stock to form a thick sauce. **7** Add the sherry, mushrooms, pear and porcini mushrooms, soaked in warm water. Bring to a simmer. **8** Whisk in the mustard and chopped tarragon, cover and cook until the pork is tender. **9** Sprinkle with the chopped walnuts and toasted breadcrumbs.

SALMON NOODLES

Super quick, super fresh, this dish is plant rich and flavoured with aromatic lemongrass.

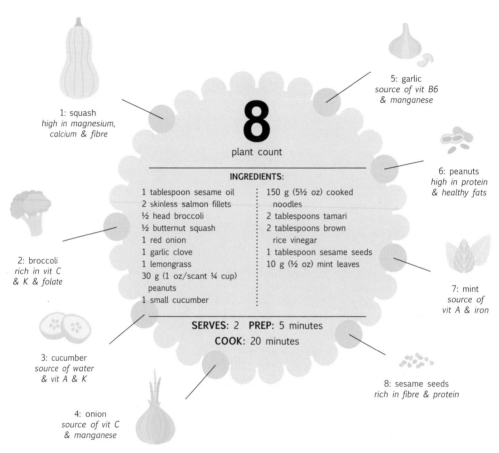

1: squash
high in magnesium, calcium & fibre

5: garlic
source of vit B6 & manganese

8
plant count

6: peanuts
high in protein & healthy fats

INGREDIENTS:

1 tablespoon sesame oil
2 skinless salmon fillets
½ head broccoli
½ butternut squash
1 red onion
1 garlic clove
1 lemongrass
30 g (1 oz/scant ¼ cup) peanuts
1 small cucumber

150 g (5½ oz) cooked noodles
2 tablespoons tamari
2 tablespoons brown rice vinegar
1 tablespoon sesame seeds
10 g (½ oz) mint leaves

2: broccoli
rich in vit C & K & folate

7: mint
source of vit A & iron

SERVES: 2 **PREP:** 5 minutes
COOK: 20 minutes

3: cucumber
source of water & vit A & K

8: sesame seeds
rich in fibre & protein

4: onion
source of vit C & manganese

METHOD:

1 Heat half the oil in a large saucepan or wok and fry the salmon, cut into bite-sized chunks for 1–2 minutes until cooked. Set aside. **2** Add the broccoli florets and squash, cut into batons, to the pan and fry for 2 minutes. **3** Add 200 ml (7 fl oz/scant 1 cup) water and cook until the water evaporates and the broccoli and squash have softened. **4** Add the remaining oil and the sliced onion and fry until soft. **5** Add the grated garlic and sliced lemongrass and stir-fry for 1 minute. **6** Add the peanuts, cucumber, shaved into ribbons, and noodles, then stir and warm through. **7** Add the salmon, tamari and vinegar and stir through for 2 minutes. Serve, sprinkled with the sesame seeds and shredded mint.

TRAYBAKES

In this chapter you will find recipes, from savoury to sweet, using just one baking tin (pan) or tray (pan). Try out these dishes as they are quick, creating punch on flavour. Turn on your oven, chop up a few plants and away you go. Simple.

BAKED OATMEAL

Baked with banana and seeds, serve these oats with a dash of milk, yoghurt or kefir of your choice. This dish only contains pecans, but mix in your favourite nuts and seeds for variety.

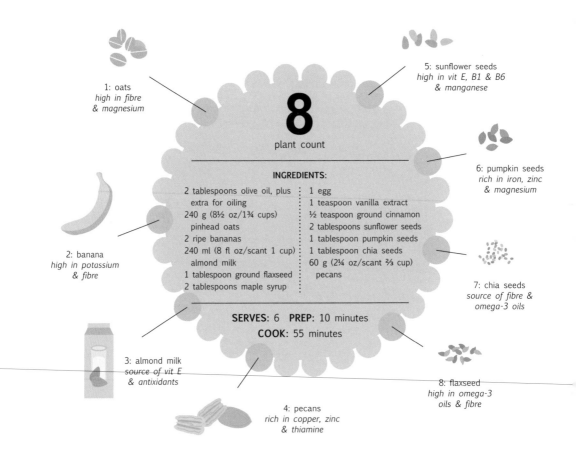

1: oats
*high in fibre
& magnesium*

5: sunflower seeds
*high in vit E, B1 & B6
& manganese*

6: pumpkin seeds
*rich in iron, zinc
& magnesium*

2: banana
*high in potassium
& fibre*

7: chia seeds
*source of fibre &
omega-3 oils*

3: almond milk
*source of vit E
& antioxidants*

4: pecans
*rich in copper, zinc
& thiamine*

8: flaxseed
*high in omega-3
oils & fibre*

8
plant count

INGREDIENTS:

2 tablespoons olive oil, plus extra for oiling
240 g (8½ oz/1¾ cups) pinhead oats
2 ripe bananas
240 ml (8 fl oz/scant 1 cup) almond milk
1 tablespoon ground flaxseed
2 tablespoons maple syrup

1 egg
1 teaspoon vanilla extract
½ teaspoon ground cinnamon
2 tablespoons sunflower seeds
1 tablespoon pumpkin seeds
1 tablespoon chia seeds
60 g (2¼ oz/scant ⅔ cup) pecans

SERVES: 6 **PREP:** 10 minutes
COOK: 55 minutes

METHOD:

1 Preheat the oven to 180°C (350°F) and oil a 23 x 23 cm (9 x 9 in) or 20 x 28 cm (8 x 11 in) baking dish. **2** Whisk the oil, oats, mashed bananas, milk, ground flaxseed, maple syrup, lightly beaten egg, vanilla, cinnamon and seeds together in a large bowl until well combined. **3** Pour the mixture into the prepared dish, cover loosely with foil and bake for 30 minutes. **4** Uncover the dish, add the pecans and bake, uncovered, for 25–30 minutes until golden brown. **5** Serve hot with yoghurt or cool, then cut into squares. Store in an airtight container for a few days.

PORRIDGE LOAF

Try this simple bread recipe for delicious slices of toast full of plant points and a creamy flavour! You can store this bread for up to three days.

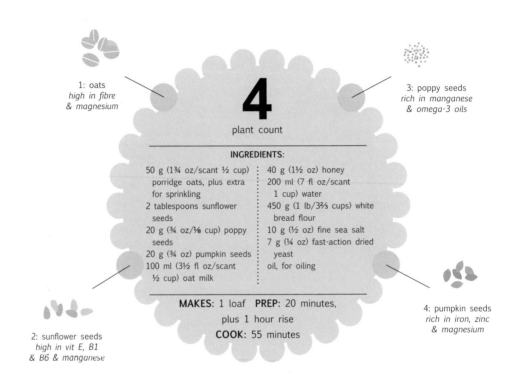

1: oats
*high in fibre
& magnesium*

4
plant count

3: poppy seeds
*rich in manganese
& omega-3 oils*

INGREDIENTS:

50 g (1¾ oz/scant ½ cup) porridge oats, plus extra for sprinkling
2 tablespoons sunflower seeds
20 g (¾ oz/⅛ cup) poppy seeds
20 g (¾ oz) pumpkin seeds
100 ml (3½ fl oz/scant ½ cup) oat milk

40 g (1½ oz) honey
200 ml (7 fl oz/scant 1 cup) water
450 g (1 lb/3⅔ cups) white bread flour
10 g (½ oz) fine sea salt
7 g (¼ oz) fast-action dried yeast
oil, for oiling

MAKES: 1 loaf **PREP:** 20 minutes, plus 1 hour rise
COOK: 55 minutes

2: sunflower seeds
*high in vit E, B1
& B6 & manganese*

4: pumpkin seeds
*rich in iron, zinc
& magnesium*

METHOD:

1 Bring the oats, seeds and milk to the boil in a saucepan. Stir in the honey, then cool. **2** To make the dough, mix the porridge mix, water, flour, salt and yeast together in a stand mixer fitted with a dough hook for 12 minutes until the dough comes away from the sides. **3** Form the dough into a ball, then put into a bowl, cover and leave in a warm place until doubled in size. **4** Preheat the oven to 210°C (410°F). **5** Oil a casserole dish (Dutch oven) or ceramic pot, shape the dough into a ball, add to the pot, dust with flour and sprinkle with oats. **6** Put into the oven, spray water six times inside oven and shut the door. **7** Bake for 40 minutes. **8** Open the oven door slightly and bake for 5 minutes to form a golden crust.

GRANOLA

A go-to nutty granola, which enhances your fruit and yoghurt breakfast any day of the week. Replace the cranberries with goji berries, raisins, sultanas (golden raisins), dried mango or apricots.

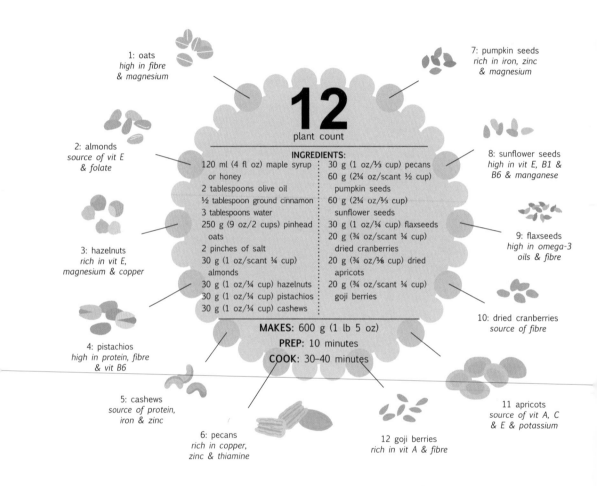

1: oats
*high in fibre
& magnesium*

7: pumpkin seeds
*rich in iron, zinc
& magnesium*

12
plant count

2: almonds
*source of vit E
& folate*

8: sunflower seeds
*high in vit E, B1 &
B6 & manganese*

3: hazelnuts
*rich in vit E,
magnesium & copper*

9: flaxseeds
*high in omega-3
oils & fibre*

4: pistachios
*high in protein, fibre
& vit B6*

10: dried cranberries
source of fibre

5: cashews
*source of protein,
iron & zinc*

11 apricots
*source of vit A, C
& E & potassium*

6: pecans
*rich in copper,
zinc & thiamine*

12 goji berries
rich in vit A & fibre

INGREDIENTS:

120 ml (4 fl oz) maple syrup or honey
2 tablespoons olive oil
½ tablespoon ground cinnamon
3 tablespoons water
250 g (9 oz/2 cups) pinhead oats
2 pinches of salt
30 g (1 oz/scant ¼ cup) almonds
30 g (1 oz/¼ cup) hazelnuts
30 g (1 oz/¼ cup) pistachios
30 g (1 oz/¼ cup) cashews

30 g (1 oz/⅓ cup) pecans
60 g (2¼ oz/scant ½ cup) pumpkin seeds
60 g (2¼ oz/⅓ cup) sunflower seeds
30 g (1 oz/¼ cup) flaxseeds
20 g (¾ oz/scant ¼ cup) dried cranberries
20 g (¾ oz/⅜ cup) dried apricots
20 g (¾ oz/scant ¼ cup) goji berries

MAKES: 600 g (1 lb 5 oz)
PREP: 10 minutes
COOK: 30–40 minutes

METHOD:

1 Preheat the oven to 150°C (300°F). **2** Heat the syrup, oil, cinnamon and water in a saucepan until runny and blended. **3** Add the remaining ingredients, except the dried fruit, to a large bowl and pour over the warm syrup. **4** Spread the mixture over two lined baking sheets and bake for 30–40 minutes stirring once halfway through, until dark golden. **5** Sprinkle with the dried fruit and cool. **6** Break into large clumps, pour into a large airtight container and store for up to three weeks.

MUFFINS

These muffins are super easy to prepare and great for a snack or light lunch packed with cheese and vegetables. Store in an airtight container for up to three days.

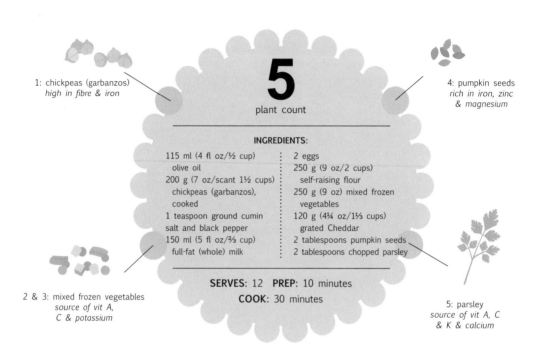

1: chickpeas (garbanzos)
high in fibre & iron

4: pumpkin seeds
rich in iron, zinc & magnesium

5
plant count

INGREDIENTS:

115 ml (4 fl oz/½ cup) olive oil	2 eggs
200 g (7 oz/scant 1½ cups) chickpeas (garbanzos), cooked	250 g (9 oz/2 cups) self-raising flour
	250 g (9 oz) mixed frozen vegetables
1 teaspoon ground cumin	120 g (4¼ oz/1⅓ cups) grated Cheddar
salt and black pepper	
150 ml (5 fl oz/⅔ cup) full-fat (whole) milk	2 tablespoons pumpkin seeds
	2 tablespoons chopped parsley

SERVES: 12 PREP: 10 minutes
COOK: 30 minutes

2 & 3: mixed frozen vegetables
source of vit A, C & potassium

5: parsley
source of vit A, C & K & calcium

METHOD:

1 Preheat the oven to 200°C (400°F). Line a 12-hole non-stick muffin tray with 12 muffin cases. **2** Heat 1 tablespoon of the oil in a frying pan, add the chickpeas and cumin and fry for 2 minutes. Season and cool. **3** Whisk the milk, eggs and remaining oil together in a large bowl until combined. Fold in the flour and season. **4** Stir in the frozen vegetables, cheese, chickpeas, pumpkin seeds and parsley, then spoon the batter into each of 12 cases. **5** Bake for 25 minutes, or until golden on top. **6** Cool for a few minutes before transferring to a wire rack. Eat while warm.

LASAGNE

A classic supper with a twist; try increasing your plant game with this beef, mushroom and pumpkin comforting pasta dish. Use any variety of pumpkin but acorn squash is particularly good.

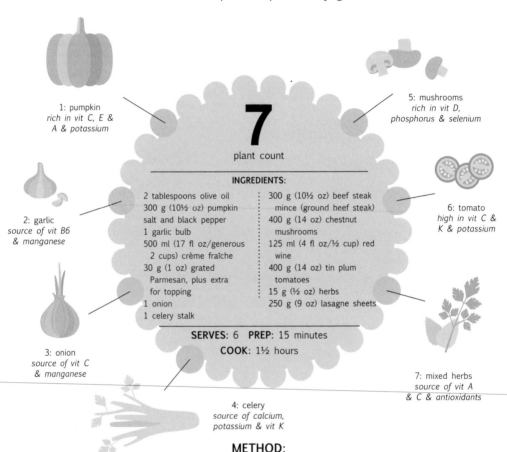

1: pumpkin
rich in vit C, E & A & potassium

5: mushrooms
rich in vit D, phosphorus & selenium

7
plant count

2: garlic
source of vit B6 & manganese

6: tomato
high in vit C & K & potassium

INGREDIENTS:

2 tablespoons olive oil
300 g (10½ oz) pumpkin
salt and black pepper
1 garlic bulb
500 ml (17 fl oz/generous 2 cups) crème fraîche
30 g (1 oz) grated Parmesan, plus extra for topping
1 onion
1 celery stalk

300 g (10½ oz) beef steak mince (ground beef steak)
400 g (14 oz) chestnut mushrooms
125 ml (4 fl oz/½ cup) red wine
400 g (14 oz) tin plum tomatoes
15 g (½ oz) herbs
250 g (9 oz) lasagne sheets

SERVES: 6 **PREP:** 15 minutes
COOK: 1½ hours

3: onion
source of vit C & manganese

7: mixed herbs
source of vit A & C & antioxidants

4: celery
source of calcium, potassium & vit K

METHOD:

1 Preheat the oven to 200°C (400°F). **2** Drizzle 1 tablespoon of the oil over the pumpkin, peeled and cut into chunks, on a baking sheet. Season. Add the foil-wrapped garlic and bake for 30 minutes. **3** Blitz the squeezed garlic and pumpkin until smooth. Mix in the crème fraîche and cheese. **4** Fry the chopped onion in the rest of the oil until soft. **5** Add the chopped celery and cook for 3 minutes. Season. **6** Add the beef and fry until browned. Add the chopped mushrooms and cook for 3 minutes. **7** Add the wine, tomatoes and herbs. Boil, then simmer for 20 minutes. **8** Layer a third of the beef in a baking dish. Cover with the pasta, then a layer of the sauce. Season. Repeat the layers two more times. Top with extra grated cheese. Bake for 45–60 minutes.

CHEESY GRATIN

Tuck into this delicious winter vegetable gratin, baked until crispy. Serve with sauerkraut to increase your plant count even more.

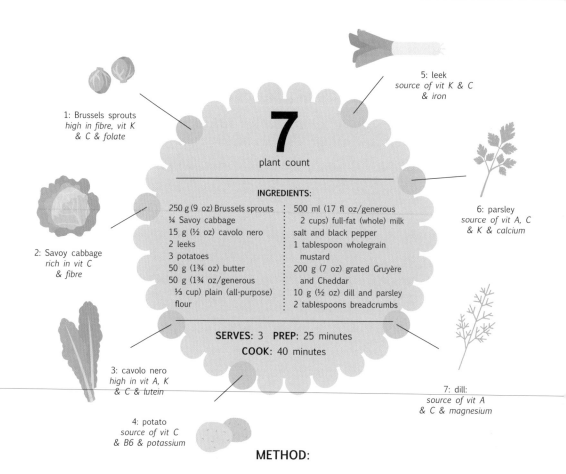

5: leek
*source of vit K & C
& iron*

1: Brussels sprouts
*high in fibre, vit K
& C & folate*

7
plant count

6: parsley
*source of vit A, C
& K & calcium*

INGREDIENTS:

250 g (9 oz) Brussels sprouts
¼ Savoy cabbage
15 g (½ oz) cavolo nero
2 leeks
3 potatoes
50 g (1¾ oz) butter
50 g (1¾ oz/generous
⅓ cup) plain (all-purpose)
flour

500 ml (17 fl oz/generous
2 cups) full-fat (whole) milk
salt and black pepper
1 tablespoon wholegrain
mustard
200 g (7 oz) grated Gruyère
and Cheddar
10 g (½ oz) dill and parsley
2 tablespoons breadcrumbs

2: Savoy cabbage
*rich in vit C
& fibre*

SERVES: 3 **PREP:** 25 minutes
COOK: 40 minutes

3: cavolo nero
*high in vit A, K
& C & lutein*

7: dill:
*source of vit A
& C & magnesium*

4: potato
*source of vit C
& B6 & potassium*

METHOD:

1 Bring a large saucepan of water to the boil. Add the halved Brussels sprouts, chopped cabbage and cavolo nero, leeks, cut into large rounds, and thinly sliced potatoes. Return to the boil and cook for 4–5 minutes. Drain and refresh under cold water. **2** Preheat the oven to 200°C (400°F). **3** Melt the butter in another pan. Stir in the flour to form a paste and cook for 2 minutes. Pour in the milk, a little at a time, and stir until the sauce thickens. Season, add the mustard, half the grated cheese and chopped herbs. Stir to combine. **4** Put the drained vegetables into an ovenproof casserole dish (Dutch oven). Pour over the sauce and mix.
5 Sprinkle with the rest of the cheese. Cover with the breadcrumbs and bake for 30 minutes until golden.

BAKED PEPPERS

This pepper dish is packed with big flavours. Serve with a crunchy green salad to increase your plant points.

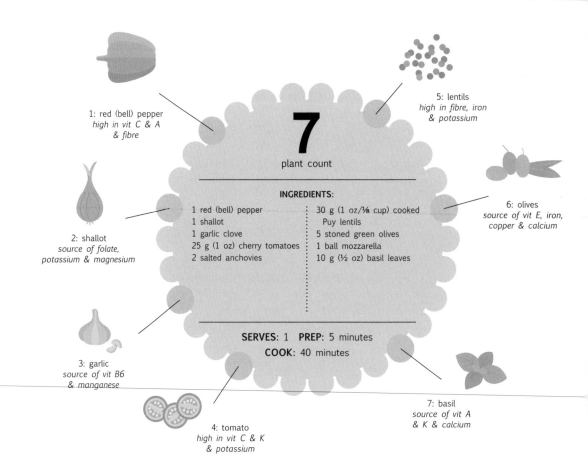

1: red (bell) pepper
*high in vit C & A
& fibre*

2: shallot
*source of folate,
potassium & magnesium*

3: garlic
*source of vit B6
& manganese*

4: tomato
*high in vit C & K
& potassium*

5: lentils
*high in fibre, iron
& potassium*

6: olives
*source of vit E, iron,
copper & calcium*

7: basil
*source of vit A
& K & calcium*

7
plant count

INGREDIENTS:

1 red (bell) pepper
1 shallot
1 garlic clove
25 g (1 oz) cherry tomatoes
2 salted anchovies

30 g (1 oz/⅛ cup) cooked
Puy lentils
5 stoned green olives
1 ball mozzarella
10 g (½ oz) basil leaves

SERVES: 1 **PREP:** 5 minutes
COOK: 40 minutes

METHOD:

1 Preheat the oven to 180°C (350°F). **2** Cut the pepper in half lengthways and remove the seeds, then arrange the pepper halves on a baking tray (pan). **3** Mix the finely sliced shallot, sliced garlic, chopped tomatoes and anchovies together, then divide the mixture between each pepper half. Bake for 30 minutes.
4 Meanwhile, mix the lentils and chopped olives together. **5** Add the olive mix to the top of each pepper half, then top with the sliced mozzarella. Bake for 10 minutes, or until the mozzarella has fully melted and is slightly golden.
6 Garnish with torn basil leaves.

BAKED LAMB

This warming lamb dish contains aubergines (eggplants) and gochujang spice, a red chilli paste from Korea. There's no need to drain the black-eyed beans, just tip the tins straight into the casserole.

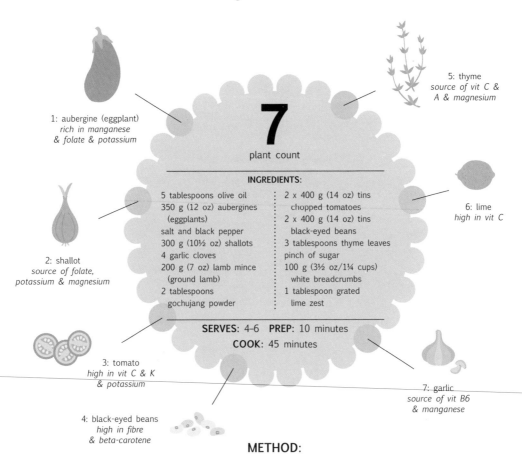

1: aubergine (eggplant)
rich in manganese & folate & potassium

2: shallot
source of folate, potassium & magnesium

3: tomato
high in vit C & K & potassium

4: black-eyed beans
high in fibre & beta-carotene

5: thyme
source of vit C & A & magnesium

6: lime
high in vit C

7: garlic
source of vit B6 & manganese

7
plant count

INGREDIENTS:

5 tablespoons olive oil
350 g (12 oz) aubergines (eggplants)
salt and black pepper
300 g (10½ oz) shallots
4 garlic cloves
200 g (7 oz) lamb mince (ground lamb)
2 tablespoons gochujang powder

2 x 400 g (14 oz) tins chopped tomatoes
2 x 400 g (14 oz) tins black-eyed beans
3 tablespoons thyme leaves
pinch of sugar
100 g (3½ oz/1¼ cups) white breadcrumbs
1 tablespoon grated lime zest

SERVES: 4-6 **PREP:** 10 minutes
COOK: 45 minutes

METHOD:

1 Rub 2 tablespoons of the oil over the aubergines, sliced into 1 cm (½ in) thick lengths, season and fry in batches on a griddle pan for 5 minutes on each side until golden brown. Set aside. **2** Preheat the oven to 200°C (400°F). **3** Heat 1 tablespoon of the oil in a casserole dish (Dutch oven) and fry the sliced shallots and chopped garlic until soft. **4** Add the lamb and fry until browned. Season. **5** Add the gochujang, tomatoes and beans. Stir in the thyme and sugar and simmer for 10 minutes. **6** Transfer the mixture to a deep 24 x 16 cm (9½ x 6¼ in) baking dish and layer up with the aubergine. **7** Mix the breadcrumbs with the lime zest and 2 tablespoons oil and sprinkle over the top. Bake for 25–30 minutes until the crumb has formed a golden crust.

FRITTATA

Discover an array of spring vegetables in this simple-to-make ricotta frittata.
It is great served with a fresh tomato salad.

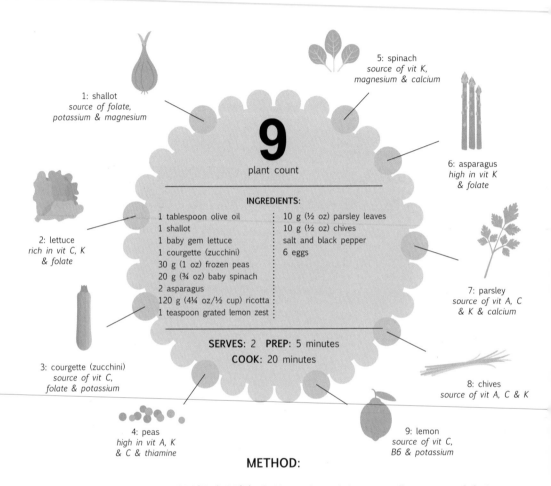

9
plant count

1: shallot
*source of folate,
potassium & magnesium*

5: spinach
*source of vit K,
magnesium & calcium*

6: asparagus
*high in vit K
& folate*

2: lettuce
*rich in vit C, K
& folate*

INGREDIENTS:

1 tablespoon olive oil
1 shallot
1 baby gem lettuce
1 courgette (zucchini)
30 g (1 oz) frozen peas
20 g (¾ oz) baby spinach
2 asparagus
120 g (4¼ oz/½ cup) ricotta
1 teaspoon grated lemon zest

10 g (½ oz) parsley leaves
10 g (½ oz) chives
salt and black pepper
6 eggs

7: parsley
*source of vit A, C
& K & calcium*

SERVES: 2 **PREP:** 5 minutes
COOK: 20 minutes

3: courgette (zucchini)
*source of vit C,
folate & potassium*

8: chives
source of vit A, C & K

4: peas
*high in vit A, K
& C & thiamine*

9: lemon
*source of vit C,
B6 & potassium*

METHOD:

1 Preheat the oven to 200°C (400°F). **2** Heat the oil in a small ovenproof frying pan and fry the sliced shallot until soft. Set aside. **3** Add the quartered lettuce to the pan and cook until each cut side is caramelised. Set aside. **4** Add the courgette, cut in half lengthways, then into slices, to the pan and fry until cooked. **5** Add the shallot, lettuce, peas, spinach and asparagus to the pan and cook for 2 minutes. **6** Whisk the ricotta, lemon zest, half the chopped herbs and seasoning together. Shape into four small balls. **7** Remove the pan from the heat and add the balls to the pan. **8** Pour over the whisked eggs and cook for 5 minutes. **9** Bake in the oven until puffed up and the ricotta is cooked. Sprinkle with the remaining herbs.

PIZZA

Discover your favourite seasonal topping using this easy pizza recipe. Use kefir in the dough instead of plain yoghurt, if you prefer.

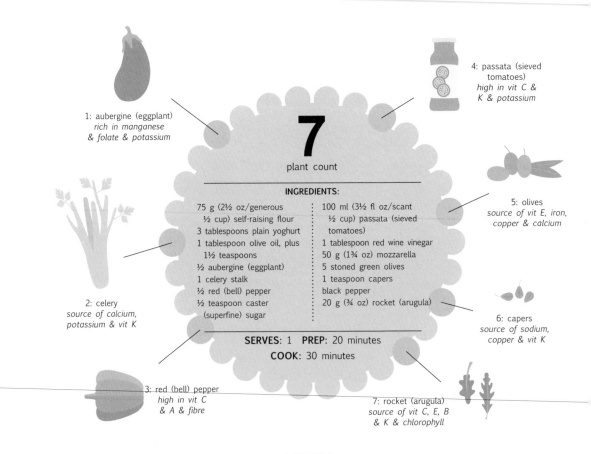

1: aubergine (eggplant)
rich in manganese
& folate & potassium

4: passata (sieved
tomatoes)
high in vit C &
K & potassium

7
plant count

INGREDIENTS:

75 g (2½ oz/generous ½ cup) self-raising flour
3 tablespoons plain yoghurt
1 tablespoon olive oil, plus 1½ teaspoons
½ aubergine (eggplant)
1 celery stalk
½ red (bell) pepper
½ teaspoon caster (superfine) sugar

100 ml (3½ fl oz/scant ½ cup) passata (sieved tomatoes)
1 tablespoon red wine vinegar
50 g (1¾ oz) mozzarella
5 stoned green olives
1 teaspoon capers
black pepper
20 g (¾ oz) rocket (arugula)

SERVES: 1   **PREP:** 20 minutes
COOK: 30 minutes

5: olives
source of vit E, iron,
copper & calcium

6: capers
source of sodium,
copper & vit K

2: celery
source of calcium,
potassium & vit K

3: red (bell) pepper
high in vit C
& A & fibre

7: rocket (arugula)
source of vit C, E, B
& K & chlorophyll

METHOD:

1 Combine the flour, yoghurt and 1½ teaspoons of the oil, then knead into a dough for 2 minutes. **2** Preheat the oven to 200°C (400°F). **3** Heat a frying pan, add the 1 tablespoon oil, then fry the aubergine, cut into cubes, until browned.
4 Add the thinly sliced celery and red pepper, cut into cubes, and fry for 3 minutes. **5** Add the sugar, passata and vinegar and cook until the sauce has reduced. **6** Roll out the dough to 15 cm (6 in) across. **7** Heat a frying pan and fry the dough for 2–3 minutes on each side. **8** Transfer to a baking tray (pan). Spread the aubergine over the top of the dough, top with the torn mozzarella, olives and capers. **9** Season with pepper and bake until the cheese has melted. Sprinkle with rocket.

CHICKEN BAKE

Cosy up with this easy chicken dish, with fennel and onions slowly roasted
in a rich chicken stock.

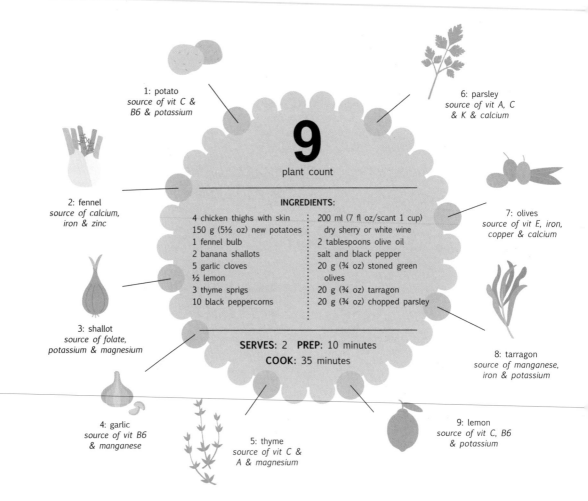

9

plant count

1: potato
*source of vit C &
B6 & potassium*

6: parsley
*source of vit A, C
& K & calcium*

2: fennel
*source of calcium,
iron & zinc*

7: olives
*source of vit E, iron,
copper & calcium*

3: shallot
*source of folate,
potassium & magnesium*

8: tarragon
*source of manganese,
iron & potassium*

4: garlic
*source of vit B6
& manganese*

5: thyme
*source of vit C &
A & magnesium*

9: lemon
*source of vit C, B6
& potassium*

INGREDIENTS:

4 chicken thighs with skin
150 g (5½ oz) new potatoes
1 fennel bulb
2 banana shallots
5 garlic cloves
½ lemon
3 thyme sprigs
10 black peppercorns

200 ml (7 fl oz/scant 1 cup)
  dry sherry or white wine
2 tablespoons olive oil
salt and black pepper
20 g (¾ oz) stoned green
  olives
20 g (¾ oz) tarragon
20 g (¾ oz) chopped parsley

SERVES: 2 **PREP:** 10 minutes
COOK: 35 minutes

METHOD:

1 Preheat the oven to 180°C (350°F). **2** Add the chicken, potatoes, quartered fennel
and shallots, garlic, quartered lemon, thyme, peppercorns and sherry to a
casserole dish (Dutch oven), then drizzle with the oil and season. **3** Bake for
35 minutes, or until the potatoes are soft and golden and the chicken is cooked
through. **4** Serve garnished with the olives, chopped tarragon leaves and parsley.

VEGETABLE STOCK

A broth to nourish your gut, it can be happily added to soups, stews and sauces, and freezes really well too.

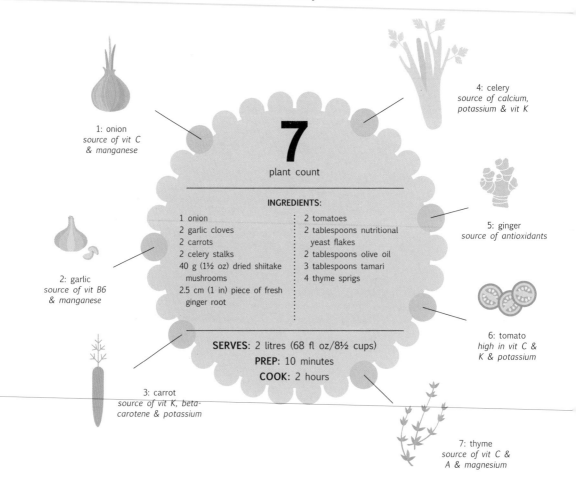

1: onion
source of vit C & manganese

4: celery
source of calcium, potassium & vit K

7

plant count

5: ginger
source of antioxidants

INGREDIENTS:

1 onion
2 garlic cloves
2 carrots
2 celery stalks
40 g (1½ oz) dried shiitake mushrooms
2.5 cm (1 in) piece of fresh ginger root

2 tomatoes
2 tablespoons nutritional yeast flakes
2 tablespoons olive oil
3 tablespoons tamari
4 thyme sprigs

2: garlic
source of vit B6 & manganese

6: tomato
high in vit C & K & potassium

SERVES: 2 litres (68 fl oz/8½ cups)
PREP: 10 minutes
COOK: 2 hours

3: carrot
source of vit K, beta-carotene & potassium

7: thyme
source of vit C & A & magnesium

METHOD:

1 Add the halved onion, garlic, chopped carrots and celery, mushrooms, sliced ginger, halved tomatoes and remaining ingredients to a large stockpot with the 2 litres (68 fl oz/8½ cups) water and bring to the boil. **2** Once boiling, reduce the heat to a simmer, cover and leave for 2 hours, stirring occasionally. **3** Cool, then strain through a sieve (fine mesh strainer). **4** Divide into glass containers. Freeze some for use later in the week and chill some in the refrigerator for immediate use. If freezing in a glass container, make sure you leave plenty of room for the liquid to expand.

FRUIT CRUMBLE

This nutty crumble is easily adaptable with the seasons. Try this autumn (fall) version using plums and pomegranate seeds, which is great served with kefir or Greek yoghurt.

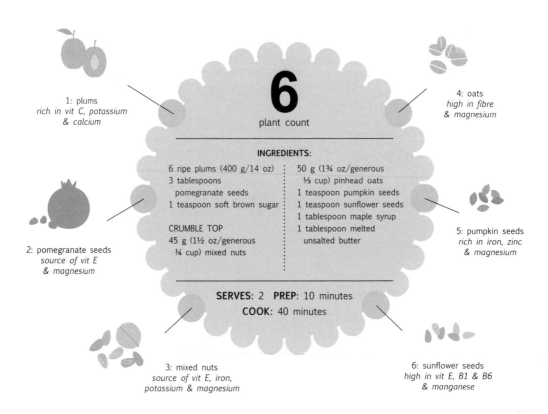

1: plums
rich in vit C, potassium & calcium

4: oats
high in fibre & magnesium

6

plant count

2: pomegranate seeds
source of vit E & magnesium

5: pumpkin seeds
rich in iron, zinc & magnesium

INGREDIENTS:

6 ripe plums (400 g/14 oz)
3 tablespoons pomegranate seeds
1 teaspoon soft brown sugar

CRUMBLE TOP
45 g (1½ oz/generous ¼ cup) mixed nuts

50 g (1¾ oz/generous ⅓ cup) pinhead oats
1 teaspoon pumpkin seeds
1 teaspoon sunflower seeds
1 tablespoon maple syrup
1 tablespoon melted unsalted butter

SERVES: 2 **PREP:** 10 minutes
COOK: 40 minutes

3: mixed nuts
source of vit E, iron, potassium & magnesium

6: sunflower seeds
high in vit E, B1 & B6 & manganese

METHOD:

1 Preheat the oven to 180°C (350°F). **2** Halve and stone the plums, then arrange them in a 30 x 20 cm (12 x 8 in) ovenproof dish with the pomegranate seeds and sprinkle with the sugar. **3** For the crumble, pulse the nuts roughly in a food processor, then add all the dry ingredients. Pour in the maple syrup and melted butter and stir to combine. **4** Sprinkle the fruits with the crumble mix, cover with foil and bake for 20 minutes. **5** Uncover and bake for a further 20 minutes, or until the fruit is soft.

APPLE GALETTE

Try and use a variety of apples for this rustic pie recipe, from Granny Smiths to Russet and Pink Ladys. They all feed your microbiome slightly differently.

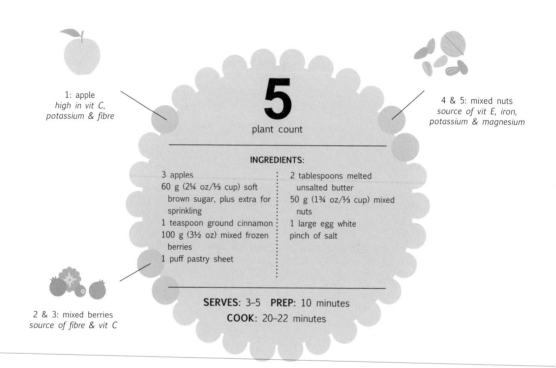

1: apple
high in vit C,
potassium & fibre

4 & 5: mixed nuts
source of vit E, iron,
potassium & magnesium

5

plant count

INGREDIENTS:

3 apples
60 g (2¼ oz/⅓ cup) soft brown sugar, plus extra for sprinkling
1 teaspoon ground cinnamon
100 g (3½ oz) mixed frozen berries
1 puff pastry sheet

2 tablespoons melted unsalted butter
50 g (1¾ oz/⅓ cup) mixed nuts
1 large egg white
pinch of salt

2 & 3: mixed berries
source of fibre & vit C

SERVES: 3–5 **PREP:** 10 minutes
COOK: 20–22 minutes

METHOD:

1 Preheat the oven to 220°C (425°F). **2** Peel, core and thinly slice the apples, about 5 mm (¼ in) thick, into a bowl. Add the sugar and cinnamon and toss to combine. **3** Let the frozen fruit thaw for 10 minutes. **4** Roll out the puff pastry if it isn't already ready rolled, then cut out a large round circle and put it onto a baking tray (pan) lined with baking parchment. **5** Brush with melted butter, then add the apples to the middle of the pastry, then the berries. **6** Sprinkle the chopped mixed nuts over the top. Fold the edge of the pastry over in 5 cm (2 in) sections,, making overlapping folds as you go. Brush with beaten egg white and sprinkle with the sugar and the salt. **7** Bake for 20–22 minutes until golden brown and bubbly.

ROCKY ROAD

This super rocky road recipe is a great snack to have on the go as it contains a variety of nuts and mixed berries to increase your plant count. Store in the refrigerator for up to a week.

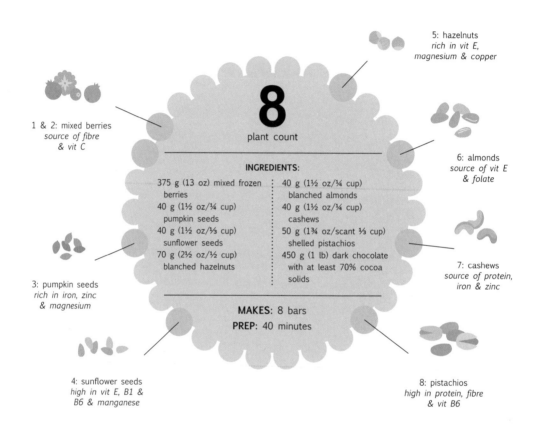

5: hazelnuts
*rich in vit E,
magnesium & copper*

1 & 2: mixed berries
*source of fibre
& vit C*

8
plant count

6: almonds
*source of vit E
& folate*

INGREDIENTS:

375 g (13 oz) mixed frozen
berries
40 g (1½ oz/¼ cup)
pumpkin seeds
40 g (1½ oz/⅓ cup)
sunflower seeds
70 g (2½ oz/½ cup)
blanched hazelnuts

40 g (1½ oz/¼ cup)
blanched almonds
40 g (1½ oz/¼ cup)
cashews
50 g (1¾ oz/scant ⅓ cup)
shelled pistachios
450 g (1 lb) dark chocolate
with at least 70% cocoa
solids

MAKES: 8 bars
PREP: 40 minutes

3: pumpkin seeds
*rich in iron, zinc
& magnesium*

7: cashews
*source of protein,
iron & zinc*

4: sunflower seeds
*high in vit E, B1 &
B6 & manganese*

8: pistachios
*high in protein, fibre
& vit B6*

METHOD:

1 Add the frozen fruit, slightly thawed, seeds and toasted nuts to a bowl.
2 Melt the chocolate, pour half over the fruit and nuts, then spread the mixture over the base of a lined 15 cm (6 in) square baking tin (pan). **3** Pour the remaining chocolate over the top and freeze for 35–40 minutes until the chocolate becomes hard. **4** Using a knife, cut into generous chunks for a great snack.

TRAIL MIX COOKIES

These cookies are very simple to make and easily adaptable using different types
of nuts, seeds and mixed dried fruit. Store in an airtight container for up
to a week.

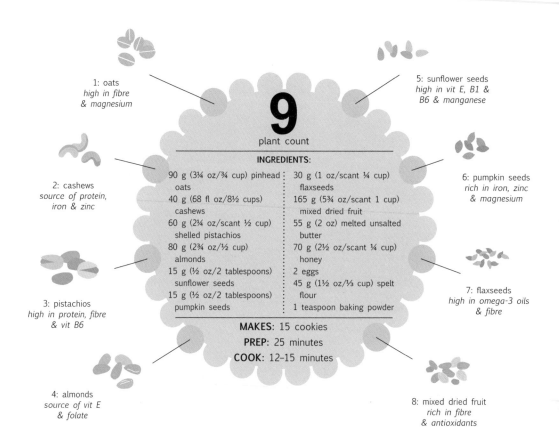

1: oats
*high in fibre
& magnesium*

5: sunflower seeds
*high in vit E, B1 &
B6 & manganese*

9
plant count

INGREDIENTS:

90 g (3¼ oz/¾ cup) pinhead oats
40 g (68 fl oz/8½ cups) cashews
60 g (2¼ oz/scant ½ cup) shelled pistachios
80 g (2¾ oz/½ cup) almonds
15 g (½ oz/2 tablespoons) sunflower seeds
15 g (½ oz/2 tablespoons) pumpkin seeds

30 g (1 oz/scant ¼ cup) flaxseeds
165 g (5¾ oz/scant 1 cup) mixed dried fruit
55 g (2 oz) melted unsalted butter
70 g (2½ oz/scant ¼ cup) honey
2 eggs
45 g (1½ oz/⅓ cup) spelt flour
1 teaspoon baking powder

2: cashews
*source of protein,
iron & zinc*

6: pumpkin seeds
*rich in iron, zinc
& magnesium*

3: pistachios
*high in protein, fibre
& vit B6*

7: flaxseeds
*high in omega-3 oils
& fibre*

MAKES: 15 cookies
PREP: 25 minutes
COOK: 12–15 minutes

4: almonds
*source of vit E
& folate*

8: mixed dried fruit
*rich in fibre
& antioxidants*

METHOD:

1 Add the oats, nuts, seeds and chopped dried fruit to a bowl. **2** Combine the
melted butter, honey and eggs together in another bowl. **3** Stir in the flour and
baking powder, then add to the oat mix and stir until combined. Leave for
15 minutes. **4** Preheat the oven to 180°C (350°F). **5** Using two large dessertspoons,
scoop one large spoonful of the mix, and using the other spoon, push the mix off
the spoon and onto one to two large baking sheets lined with baking parchment.
6 Use two wet fingers to flatten any parts of the dough that might be raised.
7 Bake for 12–15 minutes. Cool on a wire rack before eating.

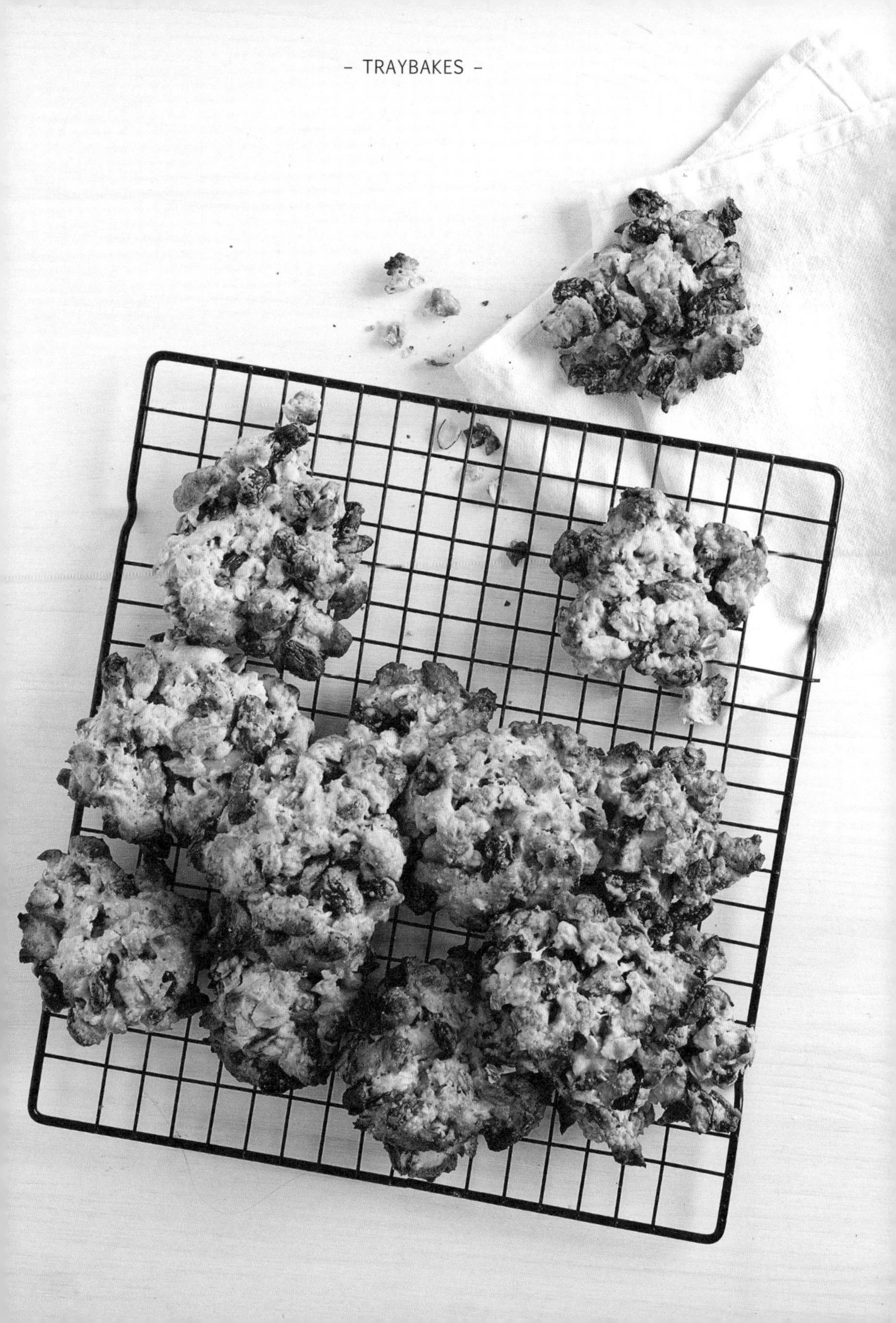

DRINKS

Creating special drinks can be a great way of adding extra plants to your diet on a daily basis. Try using fresh and frozen fruit and vegetables to keep diverse options at home. Hot milk drinks and fruity shakes are delicious ways to create a heavy plant food snack or breakfast on the go.

OAT SMOOTHIE

Start the day with this delicious high-protein and high-fibre smoothie using raw
cashews and coconut milk.

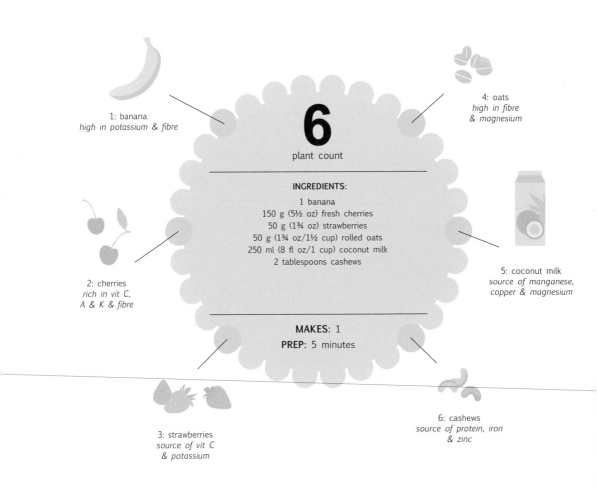

1: banana
high in potassium & fibre

4: oats
*high in fibre
& magnesium*

6

plant count

INGREDIENTS:

1 banana
150 g (5½ oz) fresh cherries
50 g (1¾ oz) strawberries
50 g (1¾ oz/1½ cup) rolled oats
250 ml (8 fl oz/1 cup) coconut milk
2 tablespoons cashews

MAKES: 1
PREP: 5 minutes

2: cherries
*rich in vit C,
A & K & fibre*

5: coconut milk
*source of manganese,
copper & magnesium*

3: strawberries
*source of vit C
& potassium*

6: cashews
*source of protein, iron
& zinc*

METHOD:

1 Add the peeled banana and stoned cherries to a blender together with the
strawberries, oats, coconut milk and cashews. **2** Whizz until smooth. Serve.

POWER SMOOTHIE

Bright and full of goodness, try this vitamin-rich drink to mix up your variety
of plants for the week ahead.

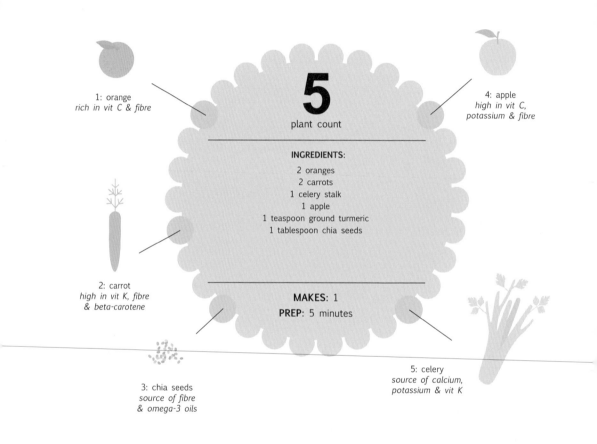

1: orange
rich in vit C & fibre

5

plant count

4: apple
*high in vit C,
potassium & fibre*

INGREDIENTS:

2 oranges
2 carrots
1 celery stalk
1 apple
1 teaspoon ground turmeric
1 tablespoon chia seeds

2: carrot
*high in vit K, fibre
& beta-carotene*

MAKES: 1
PREP: 5 minutes

3: chia seeds
*source of fibre
& omega-3 oils*

5: celery
*source of calcium,
potassium & vit K*

METHOD:

1 Add the chopped oranges, carrots, celery and apple to a blender together with
the turmeric, chia seeds and 300 ml (10 fl oz/1¼ cups) water. **2** Blitz until
smooth, adding more water, if liked, then serve.

MORNING SMOOTHIE

Wake up with this super fibre smoothie, and look after your gut. Use natural yoghurt instead of kefir, if you prefer.

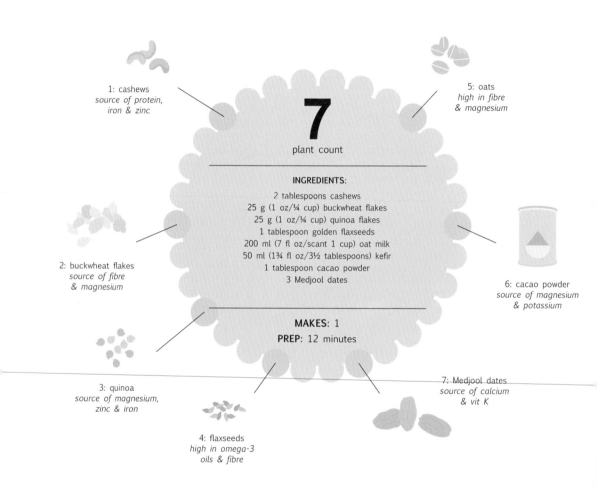

1: cashews
*source of protein,
iron & zinc*

5: oats
*high in fibre
& magnesium*

7
plant count

INGREDIENTS:

2 tablespoons cashews
25 g (1 oz/¼ cup) buckwheat flakes
25 g (1 oz/¼ cup) quinoa flakes
1 tablespoon golden flaxseeds
200 ml (7 fl oz/scant 1 cup) oat milk
50 ml (1¾ fl oz/3½ tablespoons) kefir
1 tablespoon cacao powder
3 Medjool dates

MAKES: 1
PREP: 12 minutes

2: buckwheat flakes
*source of fibre
& magnesium*

6: cacao powder
*source of magnesium
& potassium*

3: quinoa
*source of magnesium,
zinc & iron*

7: Medjool dates
*source of calcium
& vit K*

4: flaxseeds
*high in omega-3
oils & fibre*

METHOD:

1 Add the cashews, flakes and flaxseeds into a bowl. **2** Cover with water and leave for 10 minutes. Ingredients should soak up the water, but if not, drain off any excess liquid. **3** Add the mixture to a blender together with the oat milk, kefir, cacao and stoned dates and whizz until smooth. Serve.

CHOCOLATE LATTE

Warm yourself up with this delicious Indian chai-inspired spiced milk drink.

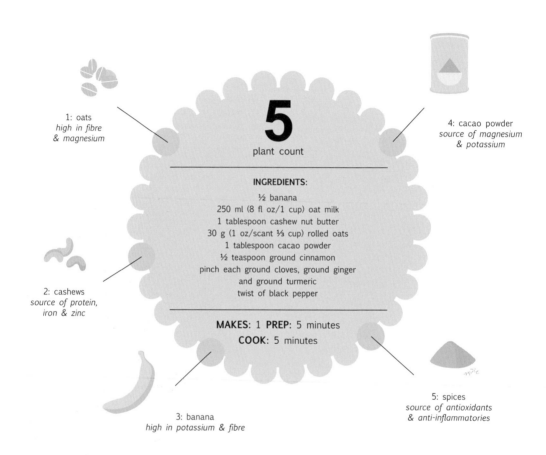

1: oats
*high in fibre
& magnesium*

5

plant count

4: cacao powder
*source of magnesium
& potassium*

INGREDIENTS:

½ banana
250 ml (8 fl oz/1 cup) oat milk
1 tablespoon cashew nut butter
30 g (1 oz/scant ⅓ cup) rolled oats
1 tablespoon cacao powder
½ teaspoon ground cinnamon
pinch each ground cloves, ground ginger
and ground turmeric
twist of black pepper

MAKES: 1 **PREP:** 5 minutes
COOK: 5 minutes

2: cashews
*source of protein,
iron & zinc*

5: spices
*source of antioxidants
& anti-inflammatories*

3: banana
high in potassium & fibre

METHOD:

1 Add the peeled banana into a blender together with remaining ingredients.
2 Blend until smooth, then pour mixture into a pan. **3** Bring to the boil, then
pour into your favourite mug.

GREEN SMOOTHIE

Drink this nine-plant smoothie in the morning to get your green fibre for the day.

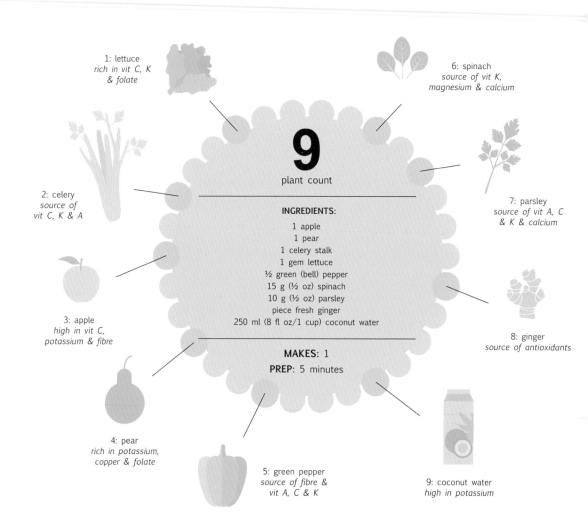

1: lettuce
rich in vit C, K & folate

6: spinach
source of vit K, magnesium & calcium

2: celery
source of vit C, K & A

7: parsley
source of vit A, C & K & calcium

3: apple
high in vit C, potassium & fibre

8: ginger
source of antioxidants

4: pear
rich in potassium, copper & folate

5: green pepper
source of fibre & vit A, C & K

9: coconut water
high in potassium

9
plant count

INGREDIENTS:

1 apple
1 pear
1 celery stalk
1 gem lettuce
½ green (bell) pepper
15 g (½ oz) spinach
10 g (½ oz) parsley
piece fresh ginger
250 ml (8 fl oz/1 cup) coconut water

MAKES: 1
PREP: 5 minutes

METHOD:

1 Add the peeled and cored apple and pear and chopped celery, lettuce and pepper to a blender together with the remaining ingredients. **2** Whizz until smooth. Serve.

SUMMER SMOOTHIE

Super fresh and zingy, try out this seasonal smoothie with the ripest fruits.
If you can't find fresh lychees, then use half a tin of lychees instead.

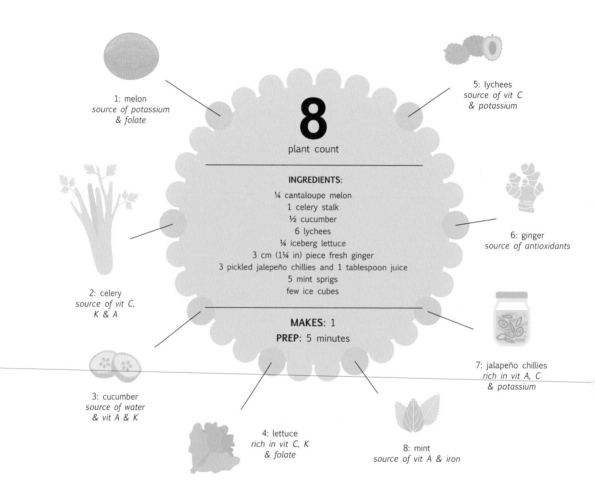

1: melon
*source of potassium
& folate*

5: lychees
*source of vit C
& potassium*

8

plant count

INGREDIENTS:

¼ cantaloupe melon
1 celery stalk
½ cucumber
6 lychees
¼ iceberg lettuce
3 cm (1¼ in) piece fresh ginger
3 pickled jalepeño chillies and 1 tablespoon juice
5 mint sprigs
few ice cubes

6: ginger
source of antioxidants

2: celery
*source of vit C,
K & A*

MAKES: 1
PREP: 5 minutes

7: jalapeño chillies
*rich in vit A, C
& potassium*

3: cucumber
*source of water
& vit A & K*

4: lettuce
*rich in vit C, K
& folate*

8: mint
source of vit A & iron

METHOD:

1 Add the seeded, skinned and chopped melon to a blender with the chopped
celery and cucumber. **2** Add peeled and stoned lychees with remaining ingredients
and 300 ml (10 fl oz/1¼ cups) water. **3** Whizz until smooth. Serve.

BEETROOT SMOOTHIE

This purple haze variety-packed smoothie is high in fibre and superfoods.
Use plain yoghurt instead of kefir, if you prefer.

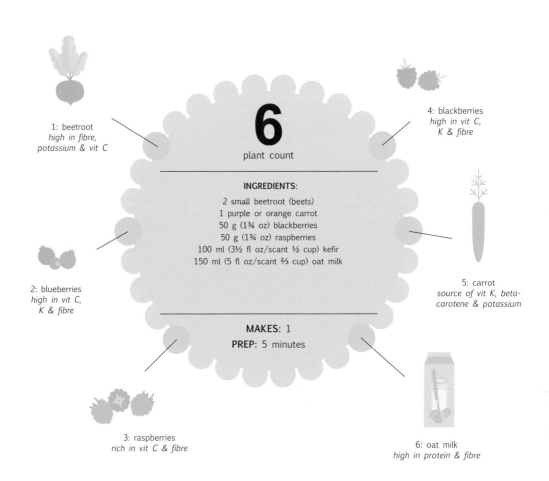

1: beetroot
*high in fibre,
potassium & vit C*

4: blackberries
*high in vit C,
K & fibre*

6

plant count

INGREDIENTS:

2 small beetroot (beets)
1 purple or orange carrot
50 g (1¾ oz) blackberries
50 g (1¾ oz) raspberries
100 ml (3½ fl oz/scant ½ cup) kefir
150 ml (5 fl oz/scant ⅔ cup) oat milk

MAKES: 1
PREP: 5 minutes

2: blueberries
*high in vit C,
K & fibre*

5: carrot
*source of vit K, beta-
carotene & potassium*

3: raspberries
rich in vit C & fibre

6: oat milk
high in protein & fibre

METHOD:

1 Put peeled and chopped beetroot and carrot into a blender with remaining
ingredients. **2** Whizz until smooth. Serve.

AVOCADO SMOOTHIE

Gut-loving avocado and lots of high-fibre vegetables, what more could you ask for in a smoothie?

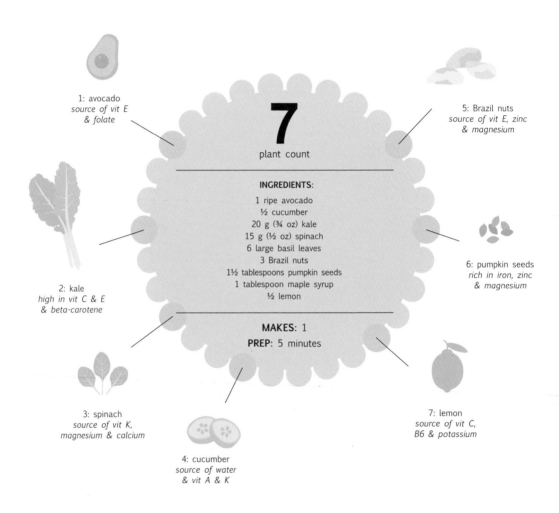

1: avocado
*source of vit E
& folate*

5: Brazil nuts
*source of vit E, zinc
& magnesium*

7

plant count

2: kale
*high in vit C & E
& beta-carotene*

6: pumpkin seeds
*rich in iron, zinc
& magnesium*

INGREDIENTS:

1 ripe avocado
½ cucumber
20 g (¾ oz) kale
15 g (½ oz) spinach
6 large basil leaves
3 Brazil nuts
1½ tablespoons pumpkin seeds
1 tablespoon maple syrup
½ lemon

MAKES: 1
PREP: 5 minutes

3: spinach
*source of vit K,
magnesium & calcium*

7: lemon
*source of vit C,
B6 & potassium*

4: cucumber
*source of water
& vit A & K*

METHOD:

1 Add the peeled and stoned avocado and chopped cucumber to a blender with remaining ingredients, lemon juice and 300 ml (10 fl oz/1¼ cups) water. **2** Whizz until smooth. Serve.

MATCHA SMOOTHIE

A popular tea blend to change up your fibre plant count using foods from the freezer. Make sure the matcha (green tea) is culinary-grade powder.

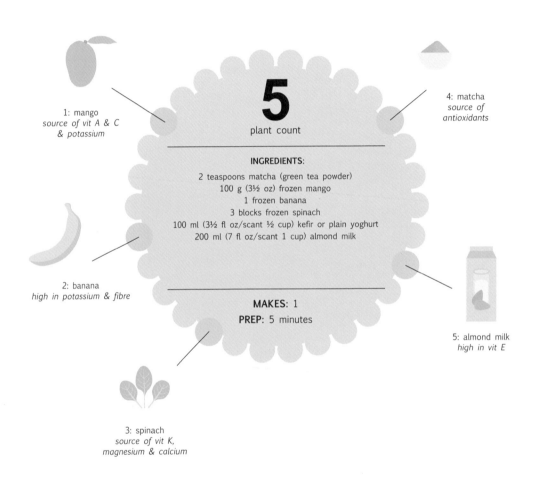

1: mango
*source of vit A & C
& potassium*

4: matcha
*source of
antioxidants*

5
plant count

INGREDIENTS:
2 teaspoons matcha (green tea powder)
100 g (3½ oz) frozen mango
1 frozen banana
3 blocks frozen spinach
100 ml (3½ fl oz/scant ½ cup) kefir or plain yoghurt
200 ml (7 fl oz/scant 1 cup) almond milk

MAKES: 1
PREP: 5 minutes

2: banana
high in potassium & fibre

5: almond milk
high in vit E

3: spinach
*source of vit K,
magnesium & calcium*

METHOD:

1 Add the ingredients to a blender. **2** Whizz until smooth. Serve.

SQUASH SMOOTHIE

This smoothie uses cooked squash, but you could use cooked pumpkin here too, if you prefer.

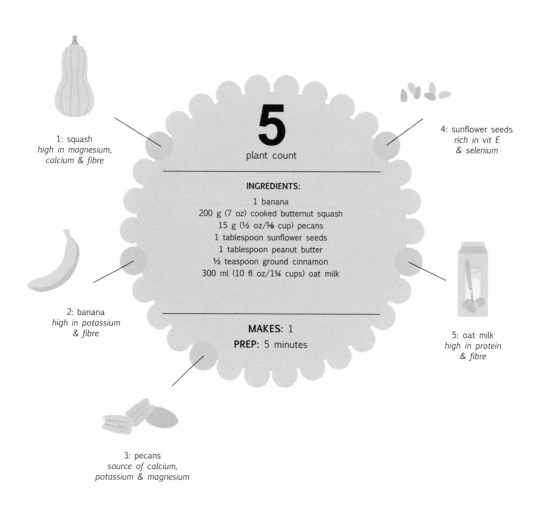

1: squash
high in magnesium, calcium & fibre

4: sunflower seeds
rich in vit E & selenium

5
plant count

INGREDIENTS:

1 banana
200 g (7 oz) cooked butternut squash
15 g (½ oz/⅛ cup) pecans
1 tablespoon sunflower seeds
1 tablespoon peanut butter
½ teaspoon ground cinnamon
300 ml (10 fl oz/1¼ cups) oat milk

MAKES: 1
PREP: 5 minutes

2: banana
high in potassium & fibre

5: oat milk
high in protein & fibre

3: pecans
source of calcium, potassium & magnesium

METHOD:

1 Add peeled or frozen banana to a blender with the remaining ingredients.
2 Whizz until smooth. Serve.

INDEX

Acknowledgements

Thank you to all the great women who helped put this book together: Kathy Steer, Alice Chadwick, Catie Ziller, Zoe Morris and Kirstie Young. In particular Zoe, who worked so hard on the photoshoot to make sure there was no food waste... a triumph!

First published in 2022 by Hachette Livre (Marabout)
This edition published in 2023 by Hardie Grant Books,
an imprint of Hardie Grant Publishing

Hardie Grant Books (London)
5th & 6th Floors
52–54 Southwark Street
London SE1 1UN

Hardie Grant Books (Melbourne)
Building 1, 658 Church Street
Richmond, Victoria 3121

hardiegrantbooks.com

British Library Cataloguing-in-Publication Data. A catalogue record for this book
is available from the British Library.

Eat More Greens
ISBN: 978-1-78488-639-4

10 9 8 7 6 5 4 3 2 1

For the Marabout edition:
Publisher: Catie Ziller
Photographer: Kirstie Young
Food Stylist: Zoe Morris
Design: Alice Chadwick
Editor: Kathy Steer

For the Hardie Grant edition:
Publishing Director: Kajal Mistry
Acting Publishing Director: Emma Hopkin
Commissioning Editor: Kate Burkett
Senior Editor: Eila Purvis
Cover designer: Stuart Hardie
Proofreader: Kathy Steer
Indexer: Cathy Heath
Production Controller: Sabeena Atchia

Colour reproduction by p2d
Printed and bound in China by Leo Paper Products Ltd.